Garden Planner

The Garden of:

Growing Season:

Introduction

Intended for use as a gardening tool, this garden planner & log book is perfect for both beginning and advanced gardeners. It is an easy to use guide for record keeping; allowing gardeners to plan for their upcoming garden season, track successes, make note of things that may not have gone as expected and plan for future success in their garden. A successful gardener learns from their experiences. From season to season and year to year, they experiment and come to discover the positive changes that can be made to help their garden grow and thrive.

The beauty of gardening is that each garden is different and ever evolving. Knowing where and how your food is grown are but a couple of the benefits of growing a personal garden. What you grow and how you grow it provides measurable results. I encourage you to expand your experience with gardening beyond the measurable results by reaching out to share and engage with your community. What you do beyond the borders of your garden provides benefits that can multiply many times over.

Lessons learned related to my gardening experiences are among the most valued lessons of my life. Patience, persistence, commitment and perseverance are but a few of the themes that have consistently woven their way through my garden. I can't thank my father enough for introducing me to the garden. The joy it brings to my life is truly beyond measure. I hope that you will find great joy in your gardening adventures as well.

A Garden Never Rests
~
It is Always Alive & Working

Stages During Each Season
In the Garden

Winter/Early Spring: Planning, Purchasing & Plot Design

Spring/Fall: Preparation of Plot(s) and Soil

Spring/Summer: Planting of Spring & Summer Crops

Spring/Summer/Fall: Pruning & Thinning

Spring/Summer/Fall: Picking of Spring & Summer Crops

Spring/Summer/Fall: Preparation, Processing & Preservation

Summer/Fall: Planting of Fall Crops

Fall: Preparing Garden to Over-Winter

Fall/Winter: Picking of Fall Crops

Fall/Winter: Post Garden Wrap-up

Considerations During Each Stage

Planning, Purchasing & Plot Design:

- Design of garden for maximum efficiency
- Research seed suppliers & generate list of seeds to purchase
- Make a list and purchase needed gardening supplies

Preparation of Plot(s) & Soil:

- Amend soil
- Weed beds
- Check watering system and make needed repairs

Planting of Spring & Summer Crops:

- Direct sow early spring crops
- Start seeds indoors, then transplant to garden
- Intercrop for maximum efficiency of garden space
- Remove spent spring crops, amend soil and plant summer crops
- Install trellises, cages, stakes, etc. for support
- Mulch

Pruning & Evaluation of Plants

- Sharpen pruning shears
- Thin plants to allow for maximum growth
- Remove suckers to maximize growth of plants
- Thin leaves to allow for good air flow & remove diseased leaves
- Apply needed resources to detract & remove garden pests
- Apply techniques for attracting pollinators

Picking of Spring & Summer Crops

- Sharpen all harvesting tools
- Clean & dry crops
- Clear storage space for crops

Preparation, Processing & Preservation

- Gather needed supplies
- Sharpen tools needed for processing
- Clean all processing & preservation equipment
- Organize storage areas
- Research & try new recipes

Planting of Fall Crops

- Prep and amend soil
- Start seeds indoors, then transplant to garden
- Direct sow fall crops
- Mulch

Preparing Garden to Over-Winter

- Compost garden debris
- Plant cover crops
- Seek out sources & gather mulch
- Apply mulch layer
- Clean & store trellises, stakes & cages

Picking of Fall Crops

- Harvest fall crops
- Research & try new recipes
- Process and store excess crops

Post Garden Wrap-up

- Note success of seed varieties
- Evaluate success of garden layout
- Research options for maximizing growing space
- Determine crop rotation for next season
- Evaluate problems in the garden & research solutions
- Research new seed varieties for next season
- Add to list of garden information resources

Soil Testing

Home Test

Name of Test _____

Where Purchased _____

Test Results

_____
_____
_____
_____
_____

Lab Test

Name of Lab _____

Contact Information for Lab

_____

Test Results

_____
_____
_____
_____

Equipment to Purchase for Growing Season

_____   _____

_____   _____

_____   _____

_____   _____

_____   _____

Supplies to Purchase for Growing Season

_____   _____

_____   _____

_____   _____

_____   _____

_____   _____

List of Compost Resources

_____   _____

_____   _____

_____   _____

_____   _____

_____   _____

If you have multiple garden beds, use this page to ketch the layout of your garden & number the beds

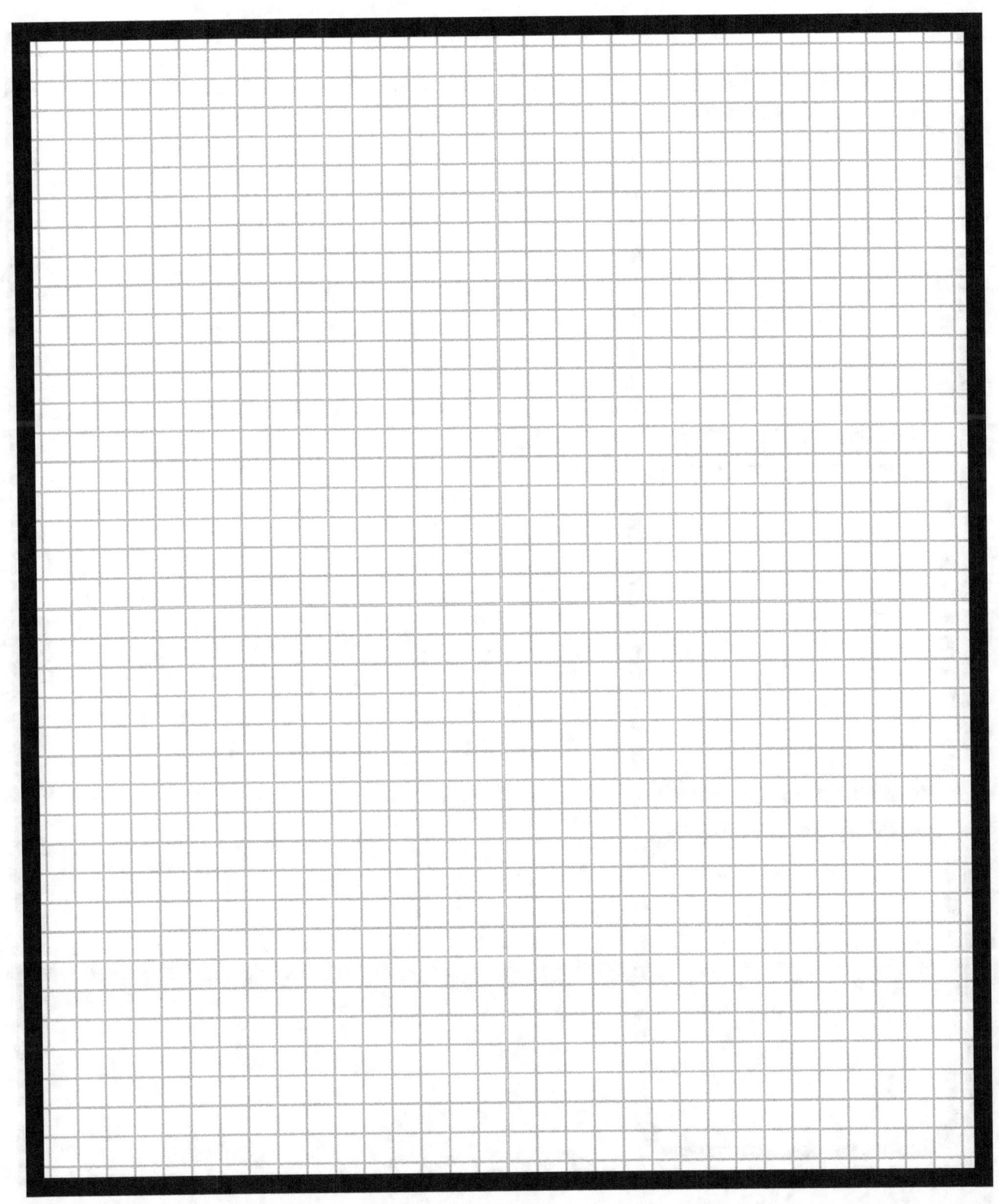

Sketch For Container Garden Plantings

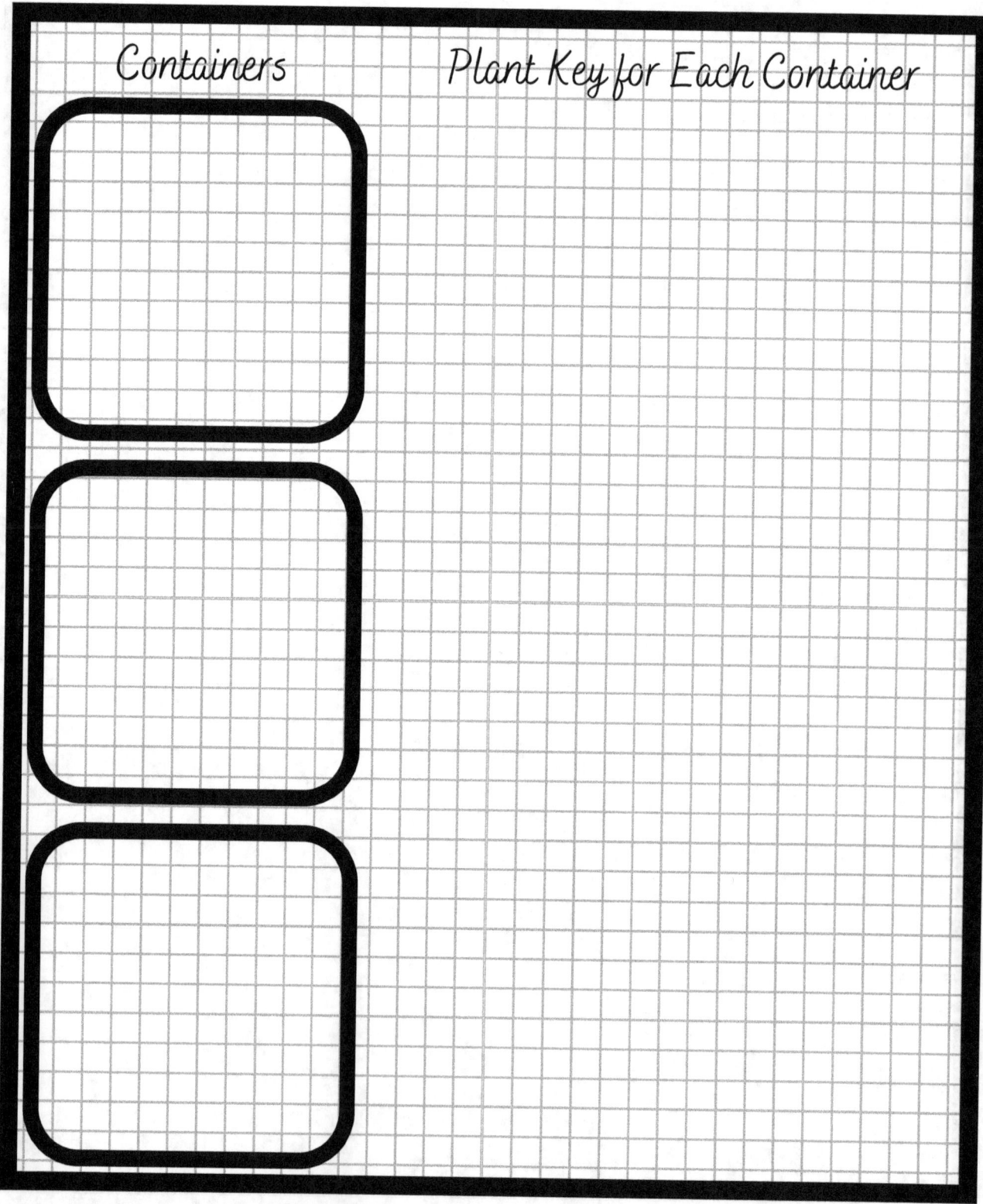

Containers

Plant Key for Each Container

Sketch For Container Garden Plantings

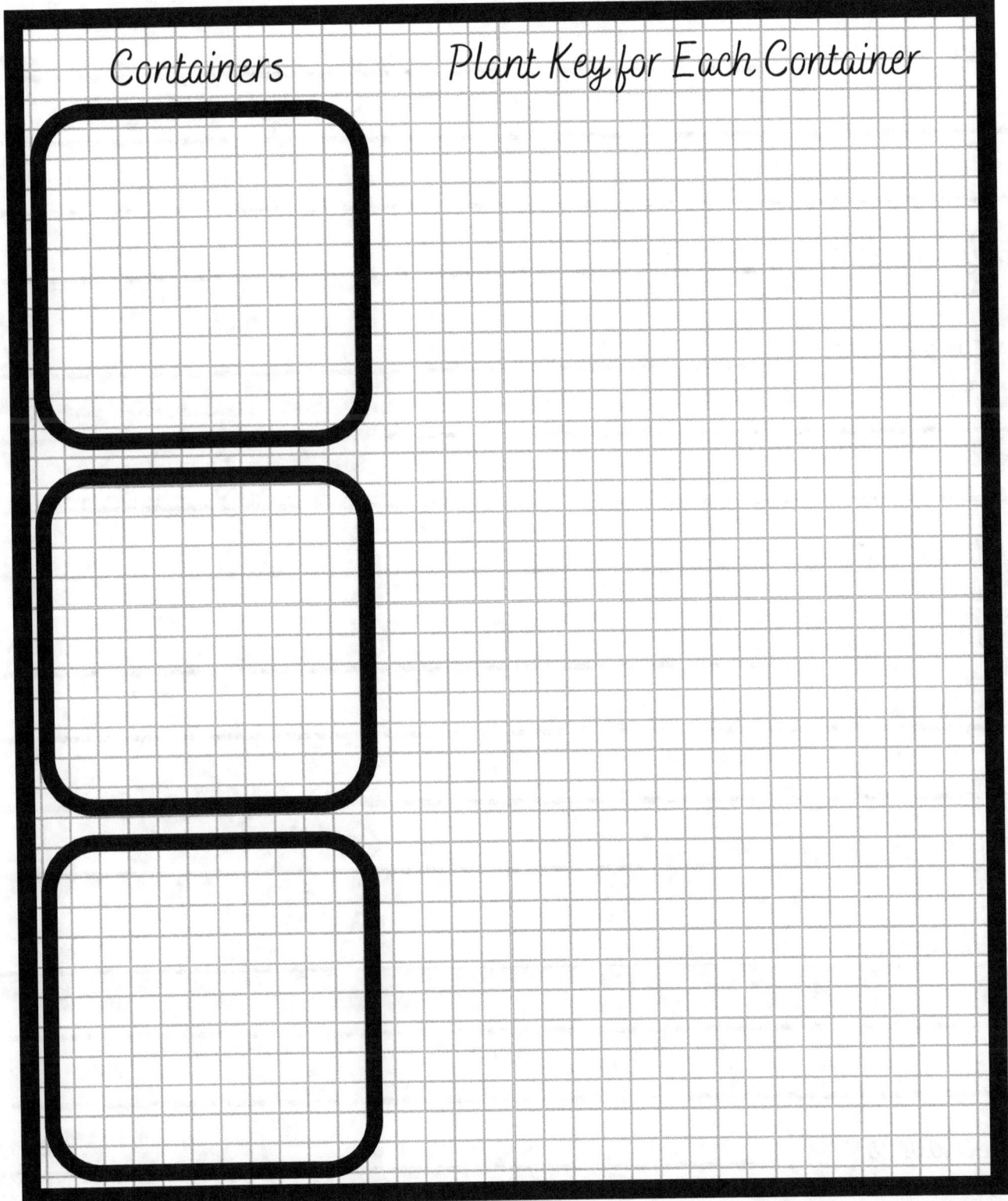

Containers

Plant Key for Each Container

List of Seed Suppliers & Their Contact Information

Seed Supplier: _____

_____

_____

Web Address: _____

Seed Supplier: _____

_____

_____

Web Address: _____

Seed Supplier: _____

_____

_____

Web Address: _____

Seed Supplier: _____

_____

_____

Web Address: _____

List of Seeds & Starts to Purchase

Varieties →

Fruits/ Herbs/ Vegetables

- ☐ Arugula
- ☐ Asparagus
- ☐ Basil
- ☐ Beans
- ☐ Beets
- ☐ Bok Choy
- ☐ Broccoli
- ☐ Brussel Sprouts
- ☐ Cabbage
- ☐ Carrots
- ☐ Cauliflower

SEEDS

List of Seeds & Starts to Purchase

Varieties →

Fruits/ Herbs/ Vegetables

☐ Celery

☐ Chard

☐ Chives

☐ Cilantro

☐ Corn

☐ Cucumbers

☐ Dill

☐ Eggplant

☐ Endive

☐ Fennel

☐ Garlic

List of Seeds & Starts to Purchase

Fruits/ Herbs/ Vegetables → **Varieties**

Fruits/Herbs/Vegetables	Varieties
☐ Gourds	
☐ Kale	
☐ Kohlrabi	
☐ Leeks	
☐ Lemongrass	
☐ Lettuce	
☐ Okra	
☐ Onions	
☐ Oregano	
☐ Parsley	

List of Seeds & Starts to Purchase

Varieties →

Fruits/ Herbs/ Vegetables

- ☐ Parsnips
- ☐ Peas
- ☐ Peppers
- ☐ Potatoes
- ☐ Pumpkins
- ☐ Radicchio
- ☐ Radishes
- ☐ Rosemary

List of Seeds & Starts to Purchase

Fruits/Herbs/Vegetables → **Varieties**

Fruits/Herbs/Vegetables	Varieties		
☐ Rutabaga			
☐ Sage			
☐ Spinach			
☐ Squash (Summer)			
☐ Squash (Winter)			
☐ Thyme			
☐ Tomatillos			
☐ Tomatoes			

SEEDS

List of Seeds & Starts to Purchase

SEEDS

Fruits/ Herbs/ Vegetables → Varieties

☐ Turnips

☐ Yams

☐ Melons

Extras

☐

☐

☐

☐

☐

Seed/Plant Variety _____

Seeds ☐   OR   Starts ☐

Seed Supplier/
Place of Purchase _____

Date Seeds Started   __ / __ / __

Quantity Planted _____

Date Starts Planted in Garden   __ / __ / __

Intercropping With _____

Garden Bed Layout/Sketch of Planting & Intercropping

Bed # _____

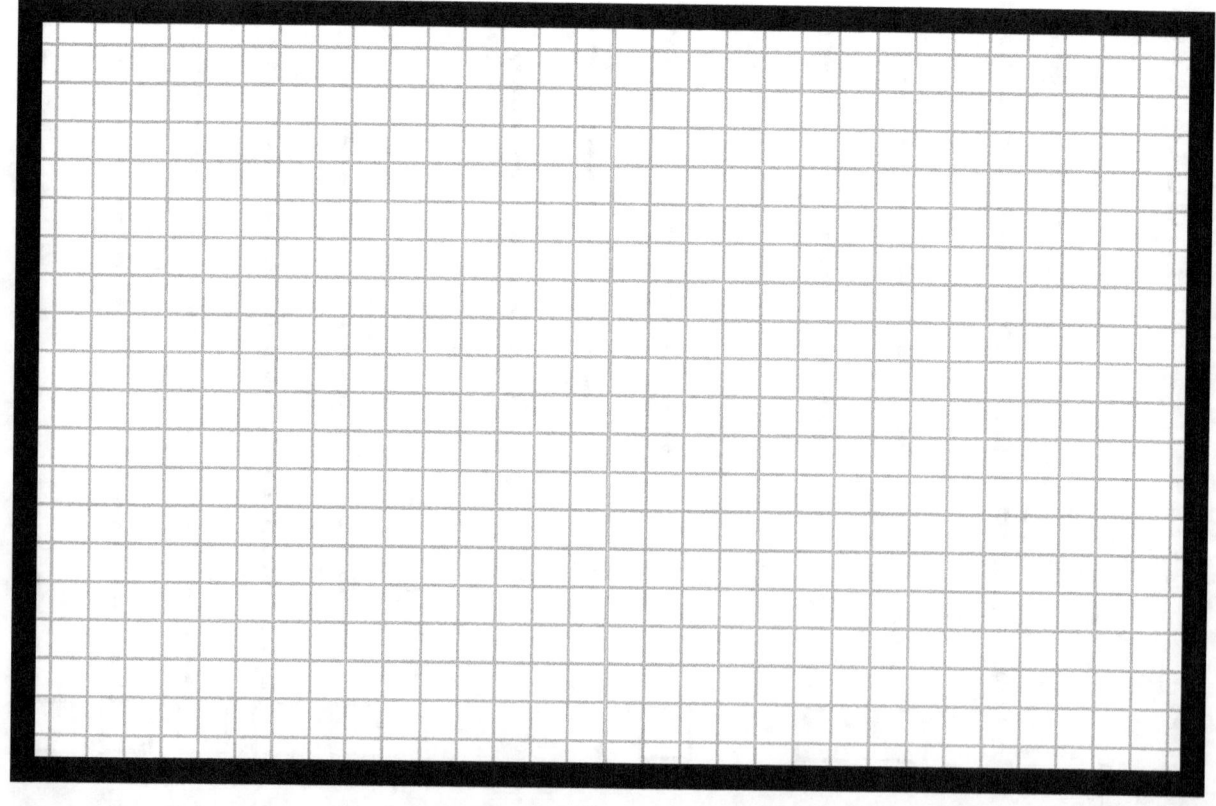

Watering Schedule   [S] [M] [T] [W] [TH] [F] [S]

Dates

Fertilize: | | | | | | | | |
|---|---|---|---|---|---|---|---|

Mulch: | | | | | | | | |
|---|---|---|---|---|---|---|---|

Prune: | | | | | | | | |
|---|---|---|---|---|---|---|---|

Date of 1st Harvest   __ / __ / __

Type of Fertilizer/Compost _____

Pest Control _____

Pruning Notes _____

_____

Success of Crop/Quantity Harvested

_____

_____

Notes Regarding Success of Planting/Suggestions for Next Year

_____

_____

Unique Challenges This Growing Season (Heat/Frost/Pests)

_____

_____

Seed/Plant Variety _____

Seeds ☐   OR   Starts ☐

Seed Supplier/

Place of Purchase _____

Date Seeds Started   __ / __ / __

Quantity Planted _____

Date Starts Planted in Garden   __ / __ / __

Intercropping With _____

Garden Bed Layout/Sketch of Planting & Intercropping

Bed # _____

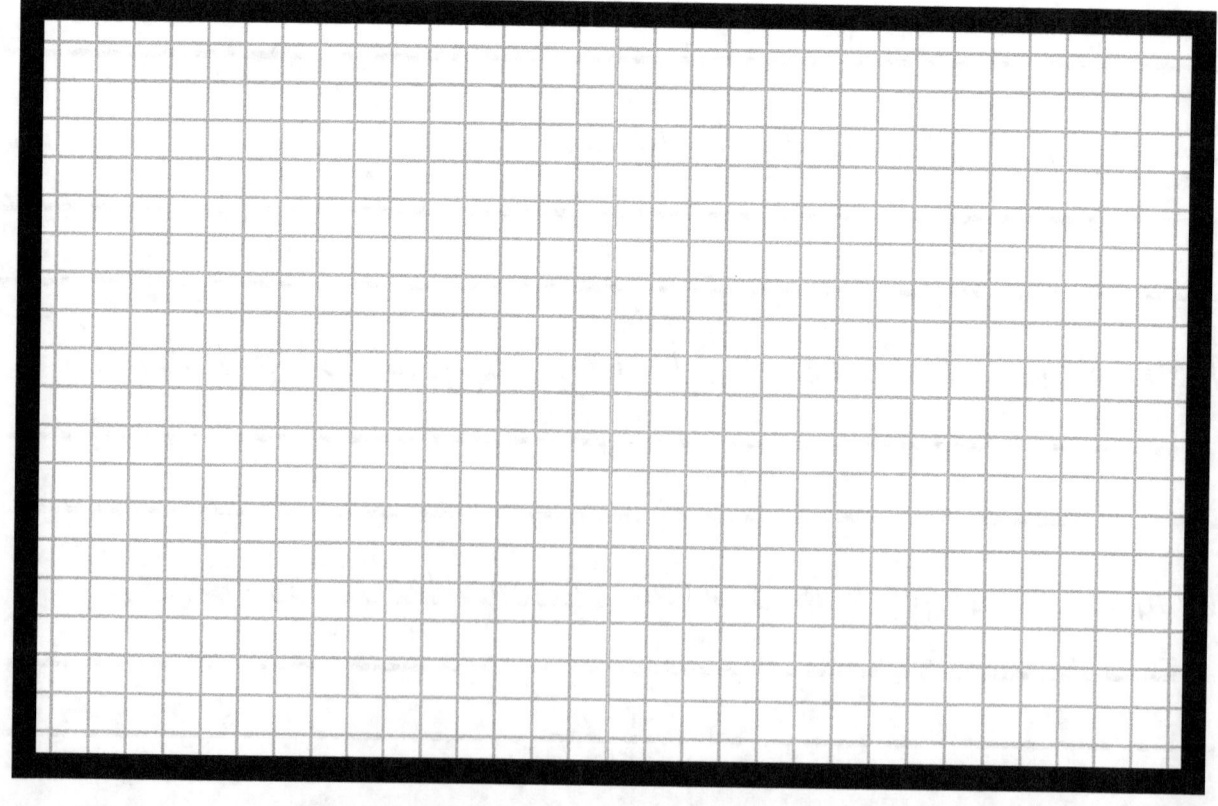

Watering Schedule   ☐ S   ☐ M   ☐ T   ☐ W   ☐ TH   ☐ F   ☐ S

Dates

Fertilize: ☐ ☐ ☐ ☐ ☐ ☐ ☐ ☐

Mulch: ☐ ☐ ☐ ☐ ☐ ☐ ☐ ☐

Prune: ☐ ☐ ☐ ☐ ☐ ☐ ☐ ☐

Date of 1st Harvest   __ / __ / __

Type of Fertilizer/Compost _____

Pest Control _____

Pruning Notes _____

_____

Success of Crop/Quantity Harvested

_____

_____

Notes Regarding Success of Planting/Suggestions for Next Year

_____

_____

Unique Challenges This Growing Season (Heat/Frost/Pests)

_____

_____

Seed/Plant Variety _____

Seeds ☐   OR   Starts ☐

Seed Supplier/
Place of Purchase _____

Date Seeds Started ___ / ___ / ___

Quantity Planted _____

Date Starts Planted in Garden ___ / ___ / ___

Intercropping With _____

Garden Bed Layout/Sketch of Planting & Intercropping
Bed # _____

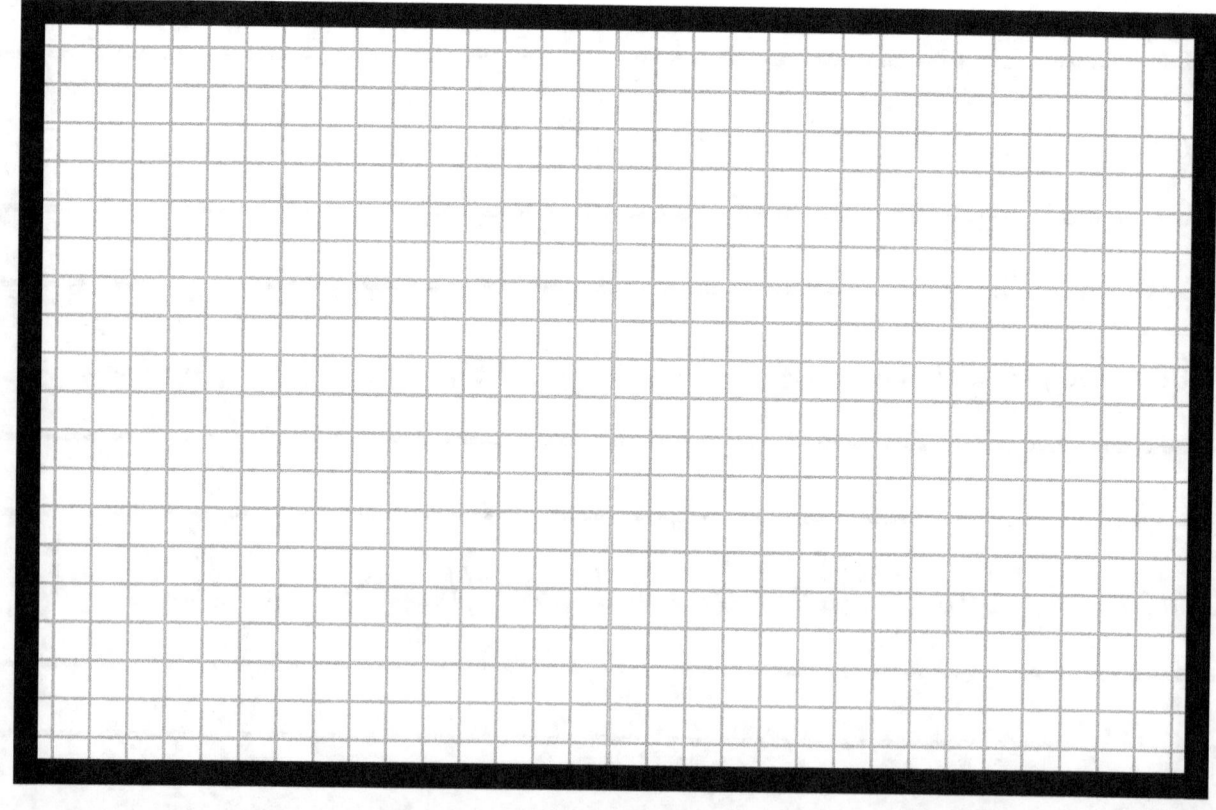

Watering Schedule   S   M   T   W   TH   F   S

Dates

Fertilize: | | | | | | | | |

Mulch: | | | | | | | | |

Prune: | | | | | | | | |

Date of 1st Harvest   __ / __ / __

Type of Fertilizer/Compost   _____

Pest Control   _____

Pruning Notes   _____

_____

Success of Crop/Quantity Harvested

_____

_____

Notes Regarding Success of Planting/Suggestions for Next Year

_____

_____

Unique Challenges This Growing Season (Heat/Frost/Pests)

_____

_____

Seed/Plant Variety _____

Seeds ☐   OR   Starts ☐

Seed Supplier/
  Place of Purchase _____

Date Seeds Started   __ / __ / __

Quantity Planted _____

Date Starts Planted in Garden   __ / __ / __

Intercropping With _____

Garden Bed Layout/Sketch of Planting & Intercropping

Bed # _____

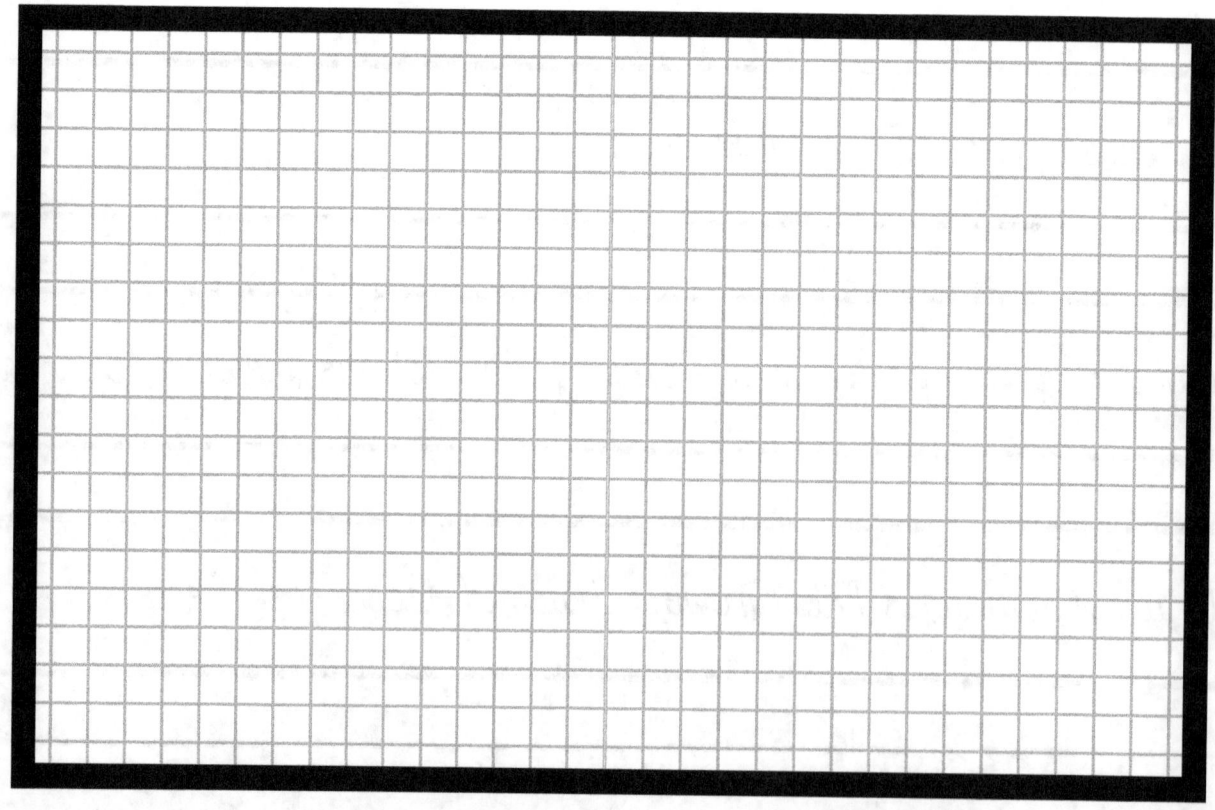

Watering Schedule   S   M   T   W   TH   F   S

Dates

Fertilize:

Mulch:

Prune:

Date of 1st Harvest   __ / __ / __

Type of Fertilizer/Compost   _____

Pest Control   _____

Pruning Notes   _____

_____

Success of Crop/Quantity Harvested

_____

_____

Notes Regarding Success of Planting/Suggestions for Next Year

_____

_____

Unique Challenges This Growing Season (Heat/Frost/Pests)

_____

_____

Seed/Plant Variety _____

Seeds ☐ OR Starts ☐

Seed Supplier/
  Place of Purchase _____

Date Seeds Started ___ / ___ / ___

Quantity Planted _____

Date Starts Planted in Garden ___ / ___ / ___

Intercropping With _____

Garden Bed Layout/Sketch of Planting & Intercropping
Bed # _____

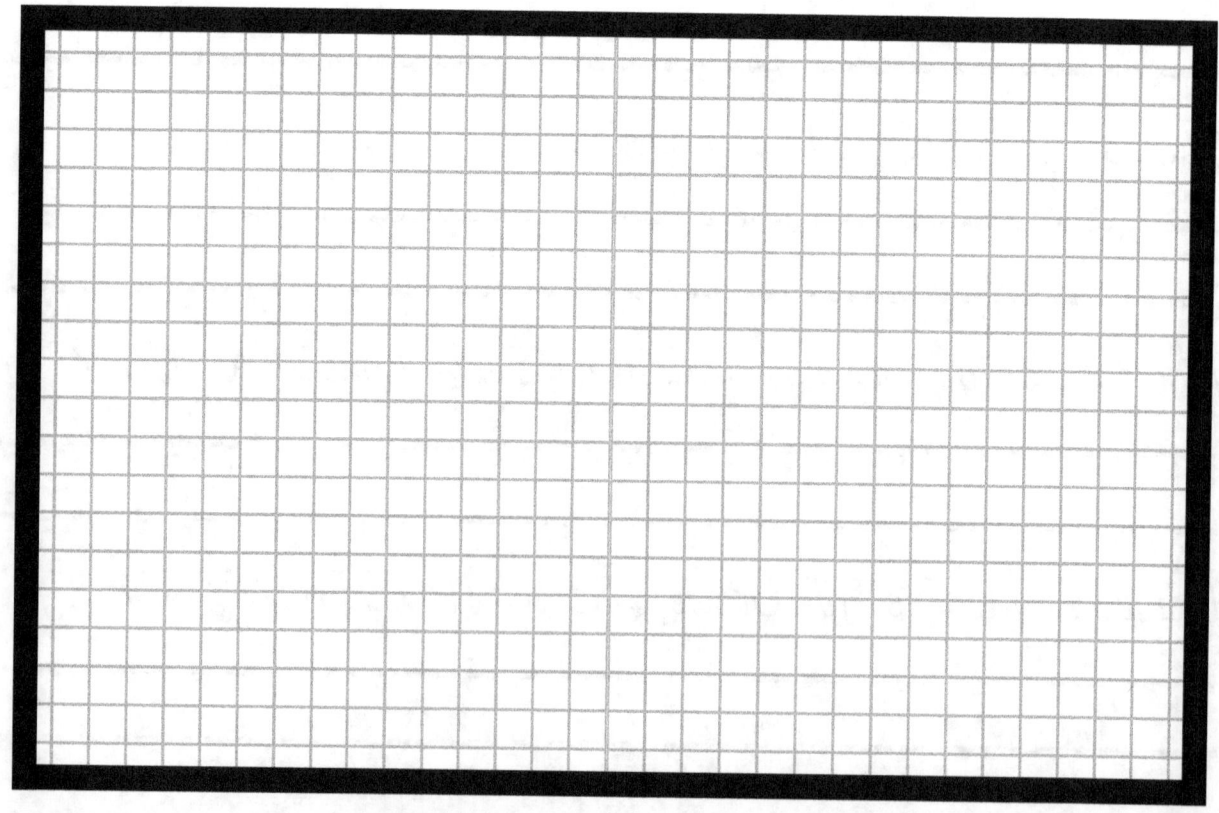

Watering Schedule   S   M   T   W   TH   F   S

Dates

Fertilize:

Mulch:

Prune:

Date of 1st Harvest   __ / __ / __

Type of Fertilizer/Compost _____

Pest Control _____

Pruning Notes _____

_____

Success of Crop/Quantity Harvested

_____

_____

Notes Regarding Success of Planting/Suggestions for Next Year

_____

_____

Unique Challenges This Growing Season (Heat/Frost/Pests)

_____

_____

Seed/Plant Variety _____

Seeds ☐   OR   Starts ☐

Seed Supplier/

Place of Purchase _____

Date Seeds Started   __ / __ / __

Quantity Planted _____

Date Starts Planted in Garden   __ / __ / __

Intercropping With _____

Garden Bed Layout/Sketch of Planting & Intercropping

Bed # _____

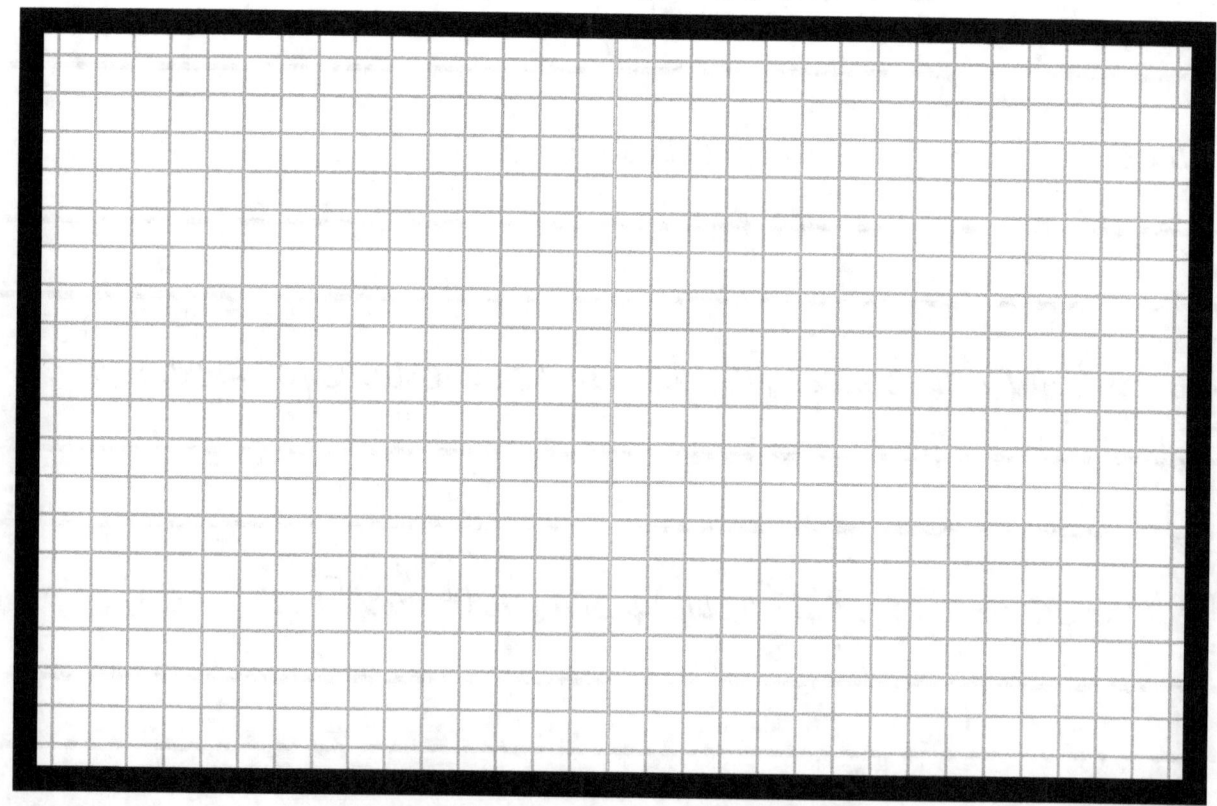

Watering Schedule | S | M | T | W | TH | F | S |

Dates

Fertilize:

Mulch:

Prune:

Date of 1st Harvest   __ / __ / __

Type of Fertilizer/Compost   _____

Pest Control   _____

Pruning Notes   _____

_____

Success of Crop/Quantity Harvested

_____

_____

Notes Regarding Success of Planting/Suggestions for Next Year

_____

_____

Unique Challenges This Growing Season (Heat/Frost/Pests)

_____

_____

Seed/Plant Variety _____

Seeds ☐   OR   Starts ☐

Seed Supplier/
   Place of Purchase _____

Date Seeds Started   __ / __ / __

Quantity Planted _____

Date Starts Planted in Garden   __ / __ / __

Intercropping With _____

Garden Bed Layout/Sketch of Planting & Intercropping

Bed # _____

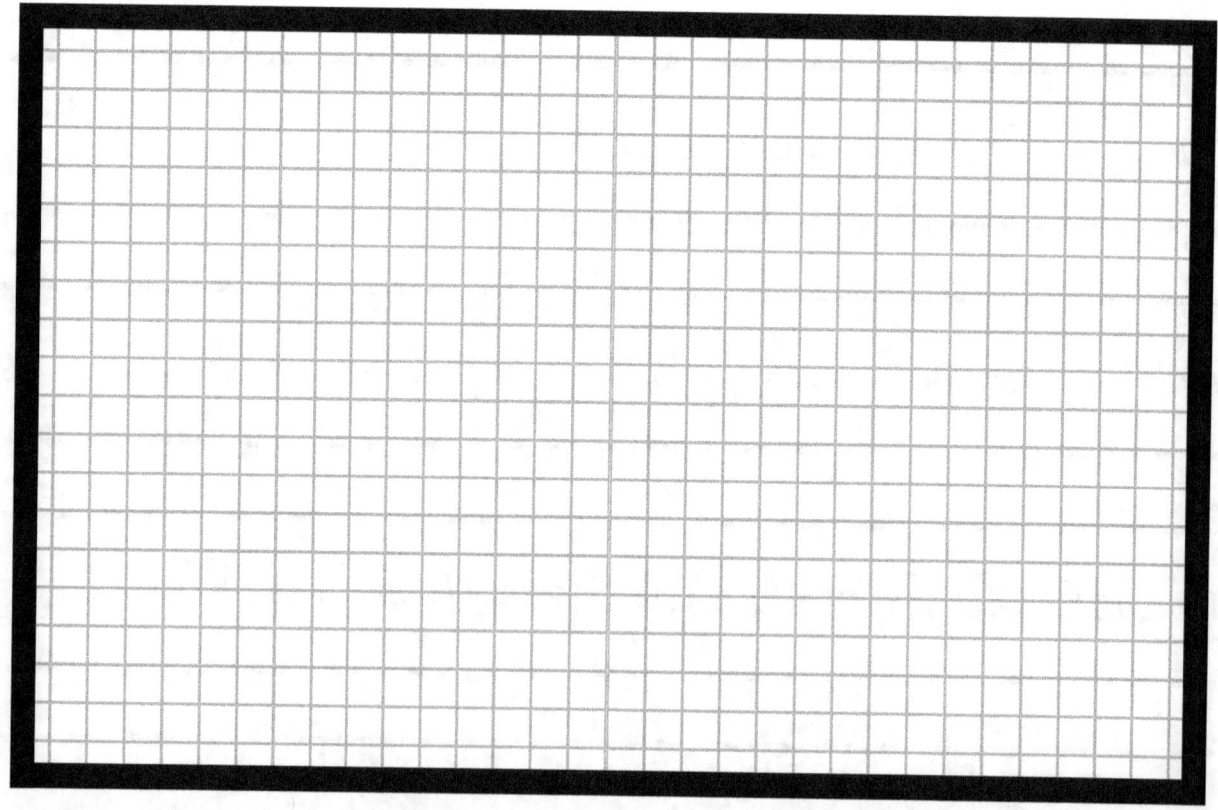

Watering Schedule   S   M   T   W   TH   F   S

Dates

Fertilize:

Mulch:

Prune:

Date of 1st Harvest   __ / __ / __

Type of Fertilizer/Compost _____

Pest Control _____

Pruning Notes _____

_____

Success of Crop/Quantity Harvested

_____

_____

Notes Regarding Success of Planting/Suggestions for Next Year

_____

_____

Unique Challenges This Growing Season (Heat/Frost/Pests)

_____

_____

Seed/Plant Variety _____

Seeds ☐   OR   Starts ☐

Seed Supplier/
  Place of Purchase _____

Date Seeds Started ___ / ___ / ___

Quantity Planted _____

Date Starts Planted in Garden ___ / ___ / ___

Intercropping With _____

Garden Bed Layout/Sketch of Planting & Intercropping

Bed # _____

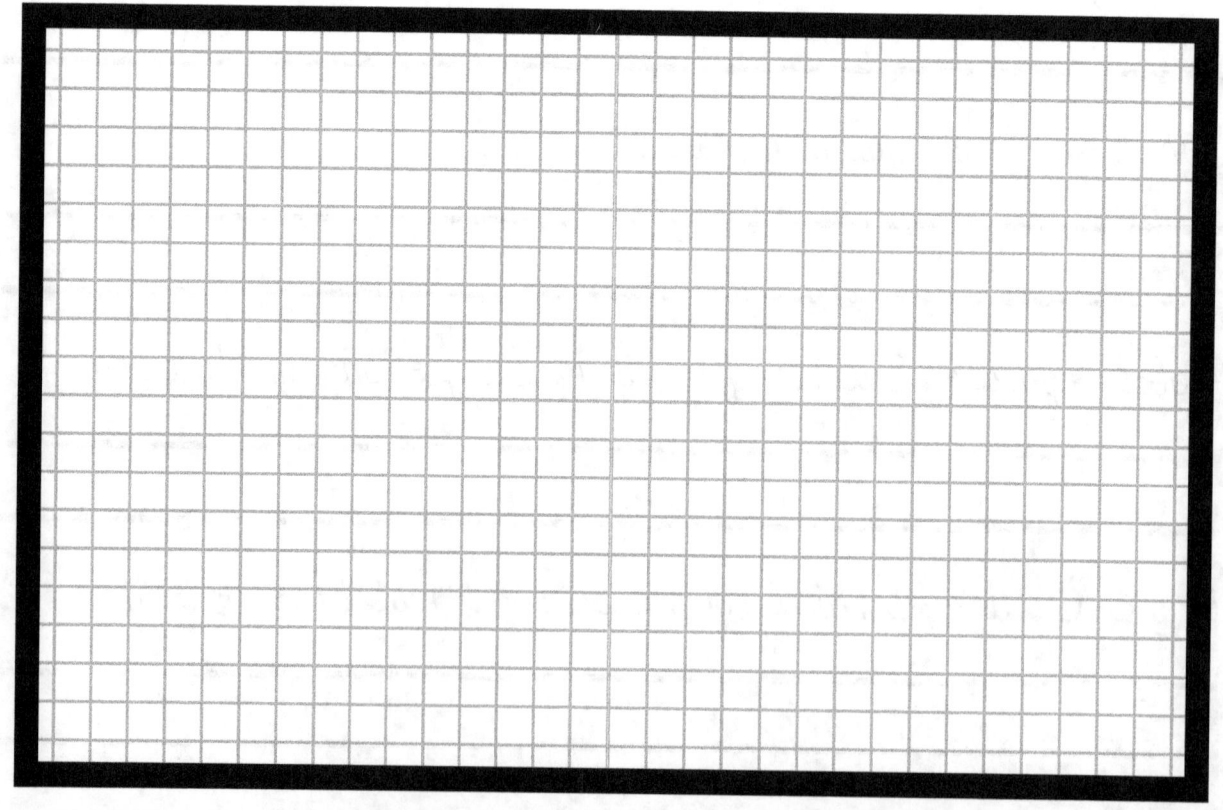

Watering Schedule S M T W TH F S

Dates

Fertilize:

Mulch:

Prune:

Date of 1st Harvest — / — / —

Type of Fertilizer/Compost _____

Pest Control _____

Pruning Notes _____

_____

Success of Crop/Quantity Harvested

_____

_____

Notes Regarding Success of Planting/Suggestions for Next Year

_____

_____

Unique Challenges This Growing Season (Heat/Frost/Pests)

_____

_____

Seed/Plant Variety _____

Seeds ☐   OR   Starts ☐

Seed Supplier/
Place of Purchase _____

Date Seeds Started   __ / __ / __

Quantity Planted _____

Date Starts Planted in Garden   __ / __ / __

Intercropping With _____

Garden Bed Layout/Sketch of Planting & Intercropping

Bed # _____

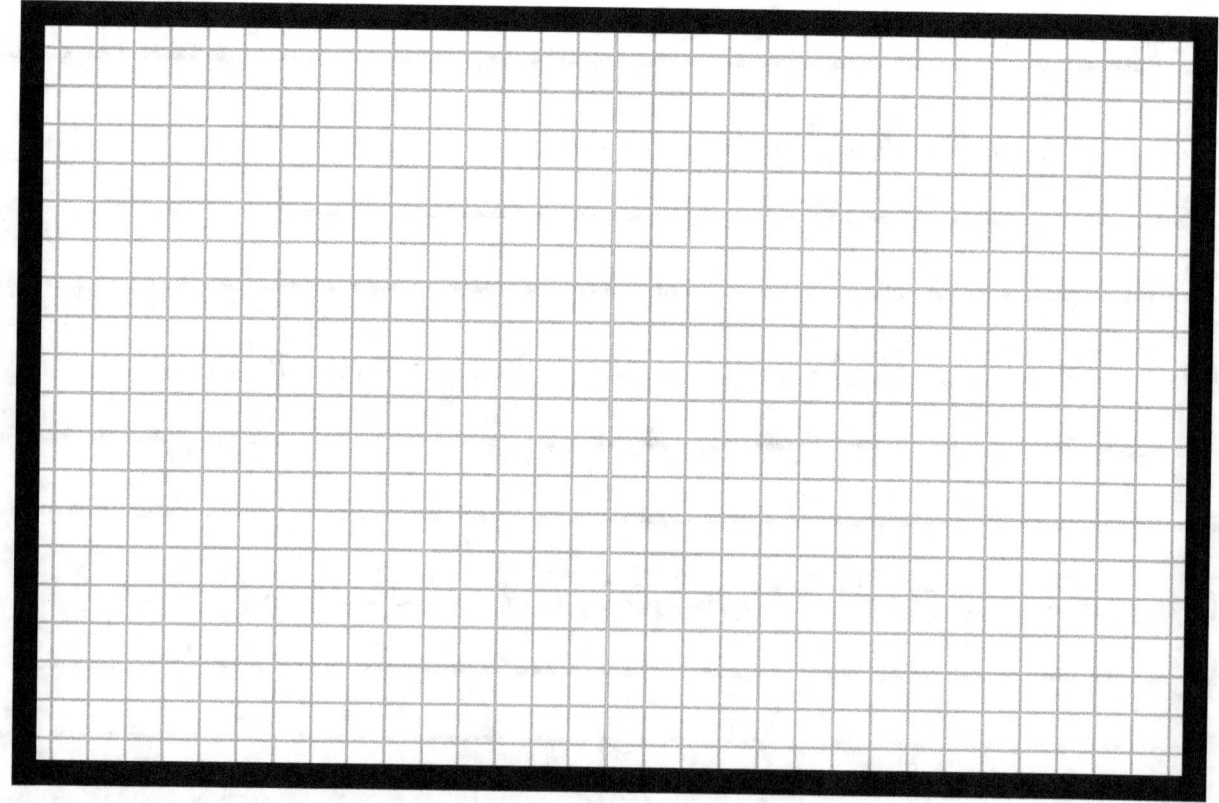

Watering Schedule   S   M   T   W   TH   F   S

Dates

Fertilize: ☐☐☐☐☐☐☐☐

Mulch: ☐☐☐☐☐☐☐☐

Prune: ☐☐☐☐☐☐☐☐

Date of 1st Harvest   __ / __ / __

Type of Fertilizer/Compost _____

Pest Control _____

Pruning Notes _____

_____

Success of Crop/Quantity Harvested

_____

_____

Notes Regarding Success of Planting/Suggestions for Next Year

_____

_____

Unique Challenges This Growing Season (Heat/Frost/Pests)

_____

_____

Seed/Plant Variety _____

Seeds ☐ OR Starts ☐

Seed Supplier/
  Place of Purchase _____

Date Seeds Started ___/___/___

Quantity Planted _____

Date Starts Planted in Garden ___/___/___

Intercropping With _____

Garden Bed Layout/Sketch of Planting & Intercropping

Bed # _____

Watering Schedule   S   M   T   W   TH   F   S

Dates

Fertilize: | | | | | | | | |
|---|---|---|---|---|---|---|---|

Mulch: | | | | | | | | |
|---|---|---|---|---|---|---|---|

Prune: | | | | | | | | |
|---|---|---|---|---|---|---|---|

Date of 1st Harvest   — / — / —

Type of Fertilizer/Compost _____

Pest Control _____

Pruning Notes _____

_____

Success of Crop/Quantity Harvested

_____

_____

Notes Regarding Success of Planting/Suggestions for Next Year

_____

_____

Unique Challenges This Growing Season (Heat/Frost/Pests)

_____

_____

Seed/Plant Variety _____

Seeds ☐   **OR**   Starts ☐

Seed Supplier/
   Place of Purchase   _____

Date Seeds Started   __/__/__

Quantity Planted   _____

Date Starts Planted in Garden   __/__/__

Intercropping With   _____

Garden Bed Layout/Sketch of Planting & Intercropping
Bed # _____

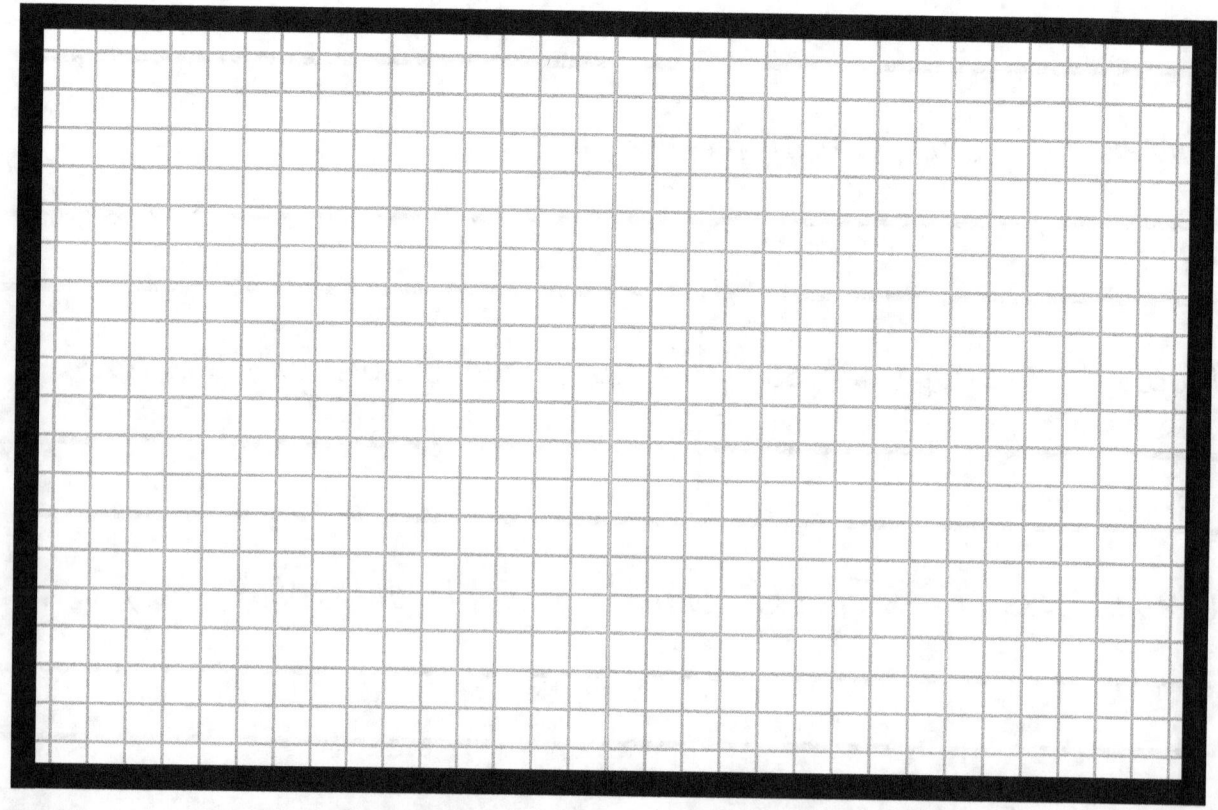

Watering Schedule S M T W TH F S

Dates

Fertilize:

Mulch:

Prune:

Date of 1st Harvest __ / __ / __

Type of Fertilizer/Compost _____

Pest Control _____

Pruning Notes _____

_____

Success of Crop/Quantity Harvested

_____

_____

Notes Regarding Success of Planting/Suggestions for Next Year

_____

_____

Unique Challenges This Growing Season (Heat/Frost/Pests)

_____

_____

Seed/Plant Variety _____

Seeds ☐ OR Starts ☐

Seed Supplier/
  Place of Purchase _____

Date Seeds Started ___ / ___ / ___

Quantity Planted _____

Date Starts Planted in Garden ___ / ___ / ___

Intercropping With _____

Garden Bed Layout/Sketch of Planting & Intercropping

Bed # _____

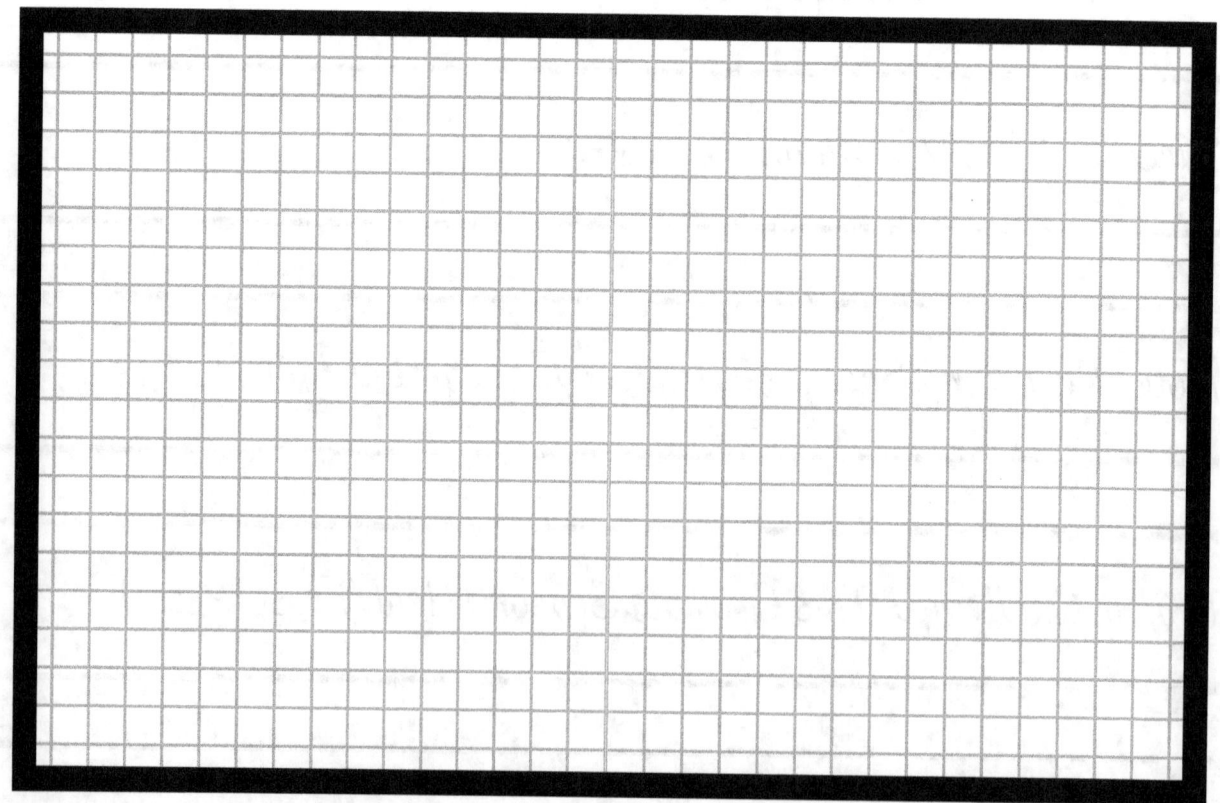

Watering Schedule | S | M | T | W | TH | F | S |

Dates

Fertilize: | | | | | | | | |

Mulch: | | | | | | | | |

Prune: | | | | | | | | |

Date of 1st Harvest — / — / —

Type of Fertilizer/Compost _____

Pest Control _____

Pruning Notes _____

_____

Success of Crop/Quantity Harvested

_____

_____

Notes Regarding Success of Planting/Suggestions for Next Year

_____

_____

Unique Challenges This Growing Season (Heat/Frost/Pests)

_____

_____

Seed/Plant Variety _____

Seeds ☐ OR Starts ☐

Seed Supplier/
  Place of Purchase _____

Date Seeds Started ___ / ___ / ___

Quantity Planted _____

Date Starts Planted in Garden ___ / ___ / ___

Intercropping With _____

Garden Bed Layout/Sketch of Planting & Intercropping

Bed # _____

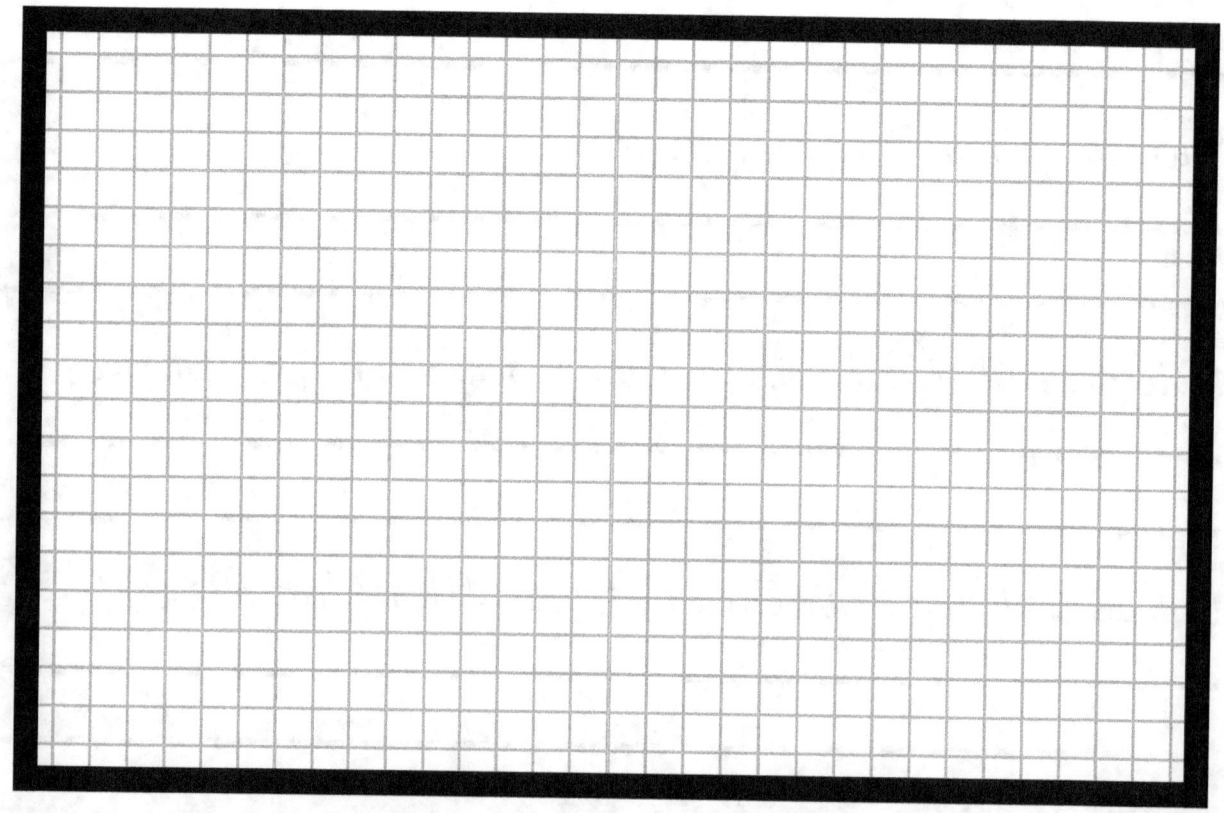

Watering Schedule | S | M | T | W | TH | F | S |

Dates

Fertilize:

Mulch:

Prune:

Date of 1st Harvest   __ / __ / __

Type of Fertilizer/Compost   _____

Pest Control   _____

Pruning Notes   _____

_____

Success of Crop/Quantity Harvested

_____

_____

Notes Regarding Success of Planting/Suggestions for Next Year

_____

_____

Unique Challenges This Growing Season (Heat/Frost/Pests)

_____

_____

Seed/Plant Variety _____

Seeds ☐   OR   Starts ☐

Seed Supplier/
  Place of Purchase _____

Date Seeds Started   __ / __ / __

Quantity Planted   _____

Date Starts Planted in Garden   __ / __ / __

Intercropping With   _____

Garden Bed Layout/Sketch of Planting & Intercropping

Bed # _____

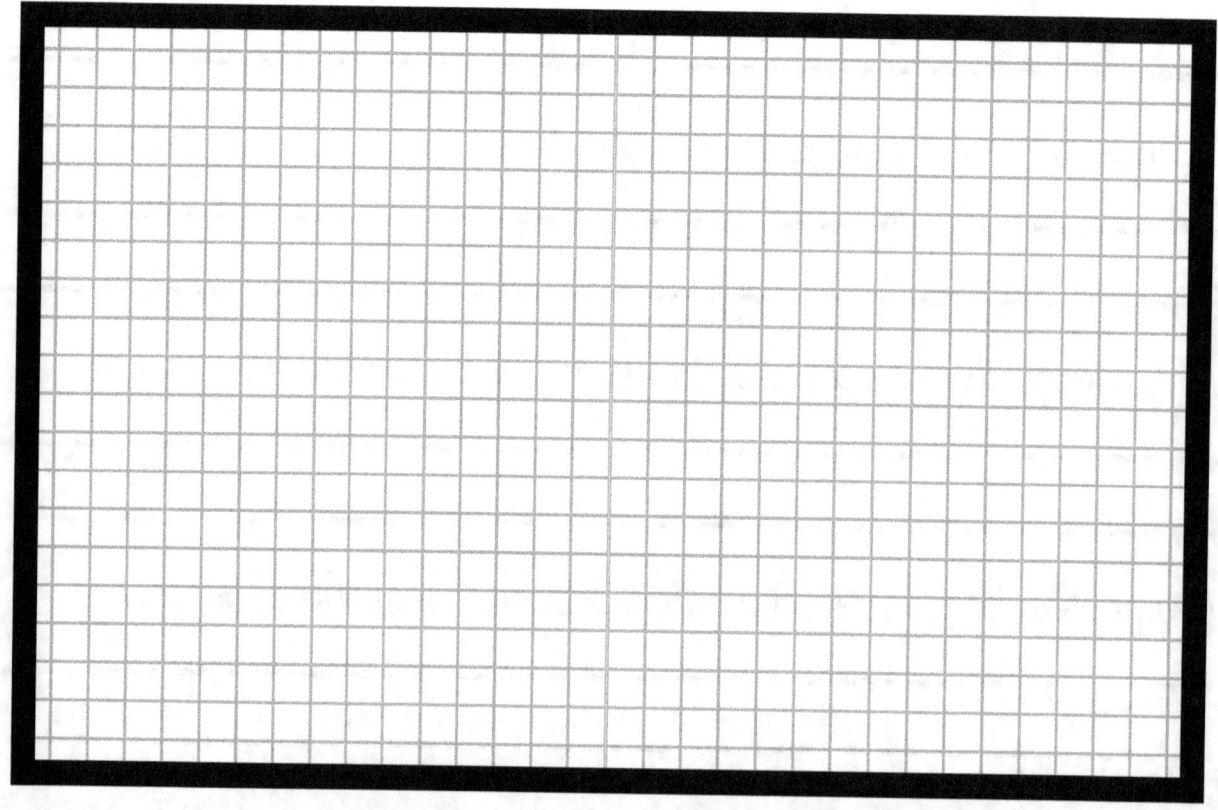

Watering Schedule | S | M | T | W | TH | F | S |

Dates

Fertilize:

| | | | | | | | |

Mulch:

| | | | | | | | |

Prune:

| | | | | | | | |

Date of 1st Harvest —— / —— / ——

Type of Fertilizer/Compost _____

Pest Control _____

Pruning Notes _____

_____

Success of Crop/Quantity Harvested

_____

_____

Notes Regarding Success of Planting/Suggestions for Next Year

_____

_____

Unique Challenges This Growing Season (Heat/Frost/Pests)

_____

_____

Seed/Plant Variety _____

Seeds ☐   OR   Starts ☐

Seed Supplier/
  Place of Purchase _____

Date Seeds Started __ / __ / __

Quantity Planted _____

Date Starts Planted in Garden __ / __ / __

Intercropping With _____

Garden Bed Layout/Sketch of Planting & Intercropping

Bed # _____

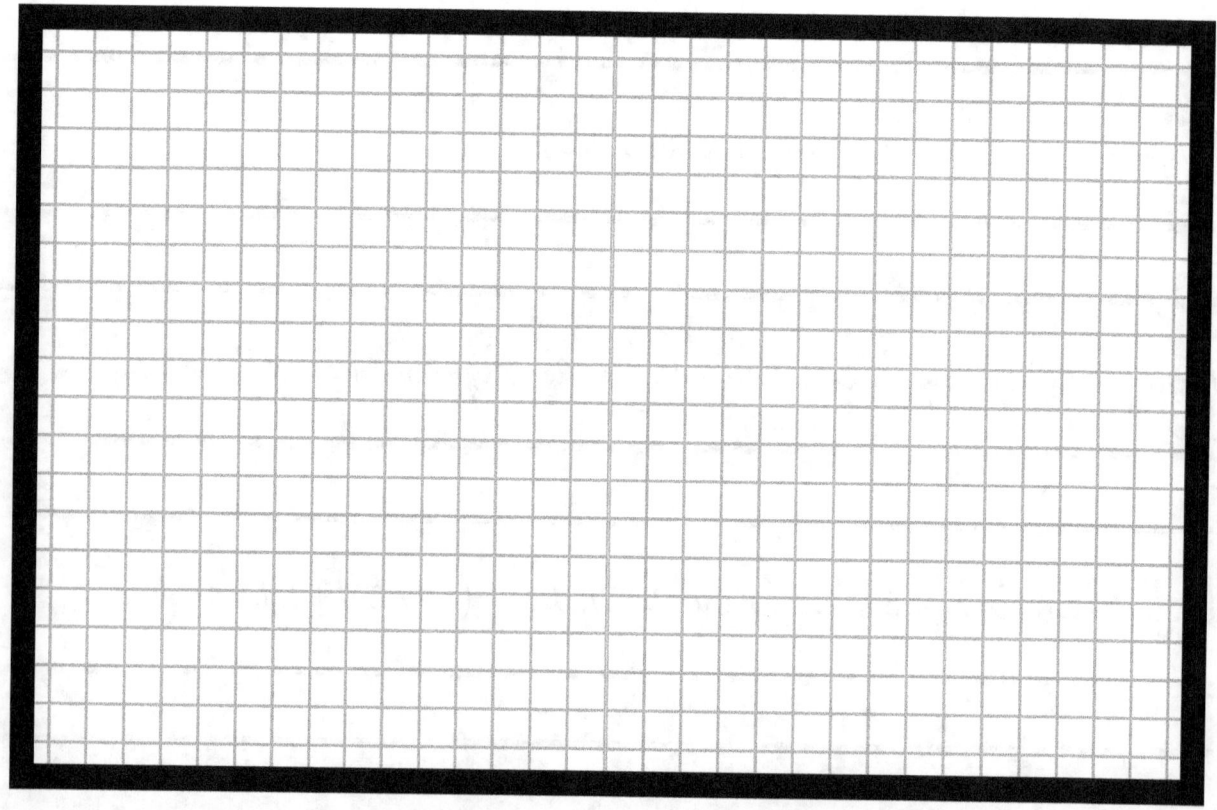

Watering Schedule | S | M | T | W | TH | F | S |

Dates

Fertilize:

Mulch:

Prune:

Date of 1st Harvest —— / —— / ——

Type of Fertilizer/Compost _____

Pest Control _____

Pruning Notes _____

_____

Success of Crop/Quantity Harvested

_____

_____

Notes Regarding Success of Planting/Suggestions for Next Year

_____

_____

Unique Challenges This Growing Season (Heat/Frost/Pests)

_____

_____

Seed/Plant Variety _____

Seeds ☐ OR Starts ☐

Seed Supplier/
  Place of Purchase _____

Date Seeds Started   __ / __ / __

Quantity Planted _____

Date Starts Planted in Garden   __ / __ / __

Intercropping With _____

Garden Bed Layout/Sketch of Planting & Intercropping

Bed # _____

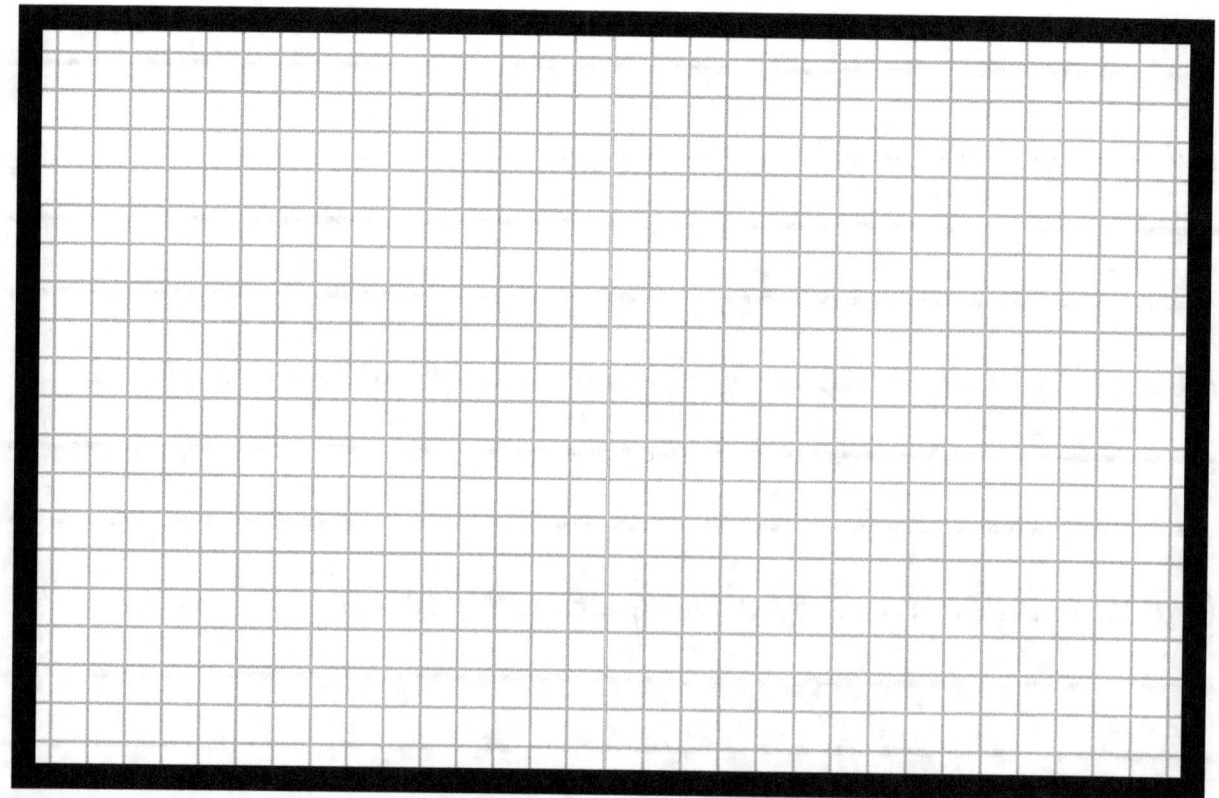

Watering Schedule   S   M   T   W   TH   F   S

Dates

Fertilize:							

Mulch:							

Prune:							

Date of 1st Harvest   __ / __ / __

Type of Fertilizer/Compost _____

Pest Control _____

Pruning Notes _____

_____

Success of Crop/Quantity Harvested

_____

_____

Notes Regarding Success of Planting/Suggestions for Next Year

_____

_____

Unique Challenges This Growing Season (Heat/Frost/Pests)

_____

_____

Seed/Plant Variety _____

Seeds ☐ OR Starts ☐

Seed Supplier/
Place of Purchase _____

Date Seeds Started ___/___/___

Quantity Planted _____

Date Starts Planted in Garden ___/___/___

Intercropping With _____

Garden Bed Layout/Sketch of Planting & Intercropping
Bed # _____

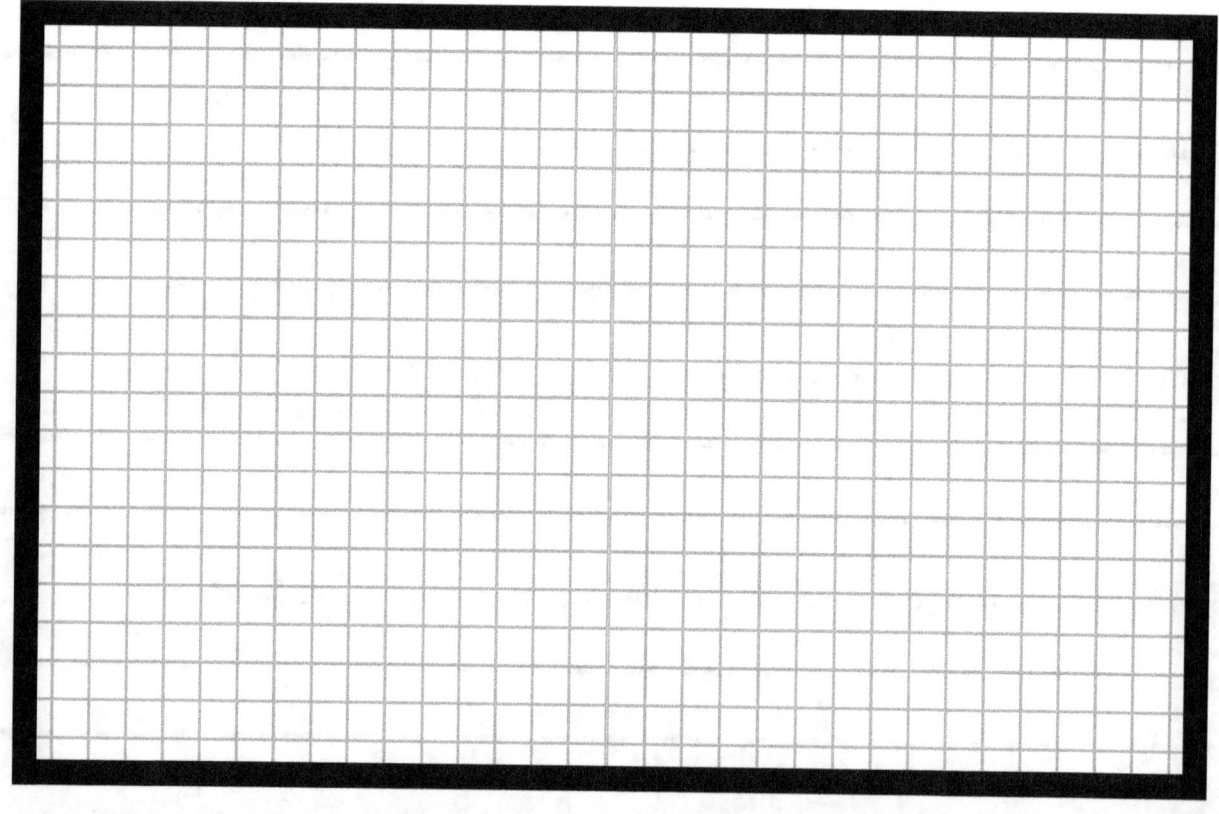

Watering Schedule S M T W TH F S

Dates

Fertilize:

Mulch:

Prune:

Date of 1st Harvest   __ / __ / __

Type of Fertilizer/Compost _____

Pest Control _____

Pruning Notes _____

_____

Success of Crop/Quantity Harvested

_____

_____

Notes Regarding Success of Planting/Suggestions for Next Year

_____

_____

Unique Challenges This Growing Season (Heat/Frost/Pests)

_____

_____

Seed/Plant Variety _____

Seeds ☐   OR   Starts ☐

Seed Supplier/
Place of Purchase _____

Date Seeds Started ___/___/___

Quantity Planted _____

Date Starts Planted in Garden ___/___/___

Intercropping With _____

Garden Bed Layout/Sketch of Planting & Intercropping
Bed # _____

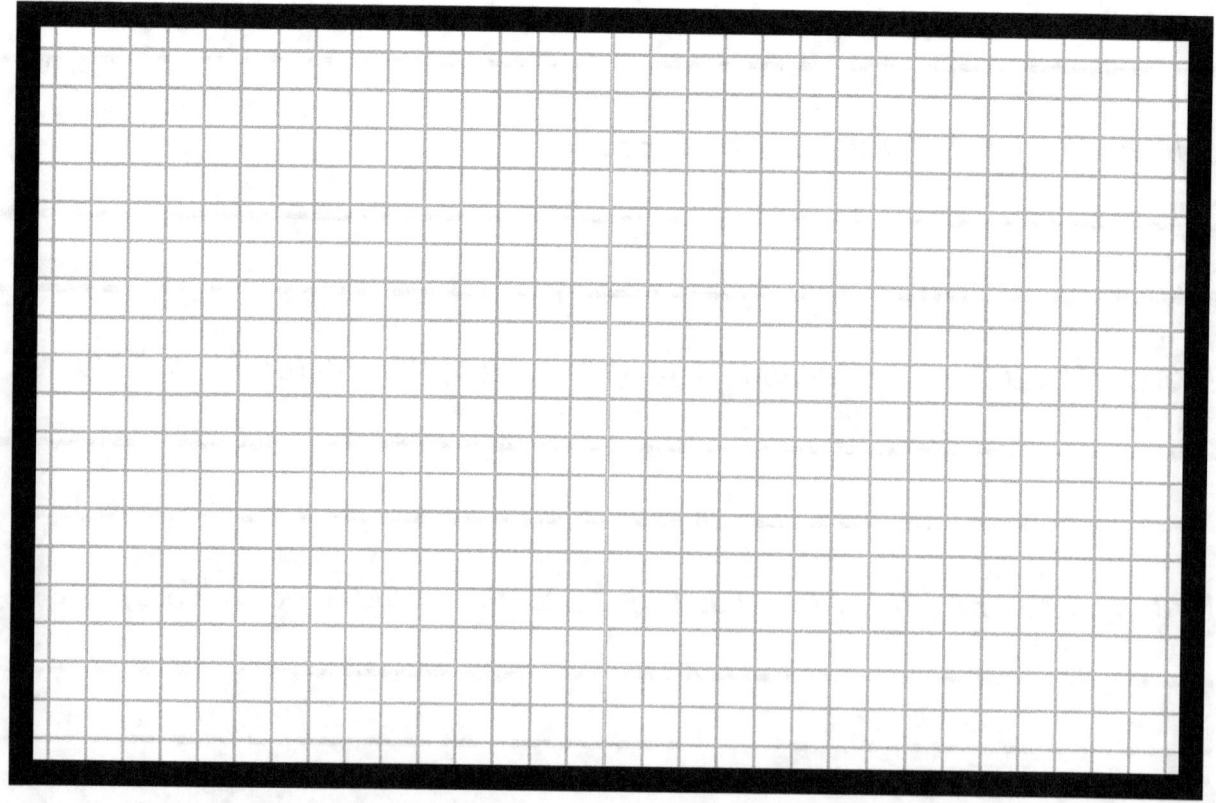

Watering Schedule $\quad$ S $\quad$ M $\quad$ T $\quad$ W $\quad$ TH $\quad$ F $\quad$ S

Dates

Fertilize:

Mulch:

Prune:

Date of 1st Harvest $\quad$ —— / —— / ——

Type of Fertilizer/Compost _____

Pest Control _____

Pruning Notes _____

_____

Success of Crop/Quantity Harvested

_____

_____

Notes Regarding Success of Planting/Suggestions for Next Year

_____

_____

Unique Challenges This Growing Season (Heat/Frost/Pests)

_____

_____

Seed/Plant Variety _____

Seeds ☐   OR   Starts ☐

Seed Supplier/
   Place of Purchase _____

Date Seeds Started ___/___/___

Quantity Planted _____

Date Starts Planted in Garden ___/___/___

Intercropping With _____

Garden Bed Layout/Sketch of Planting & Intercropping

Bed # _____

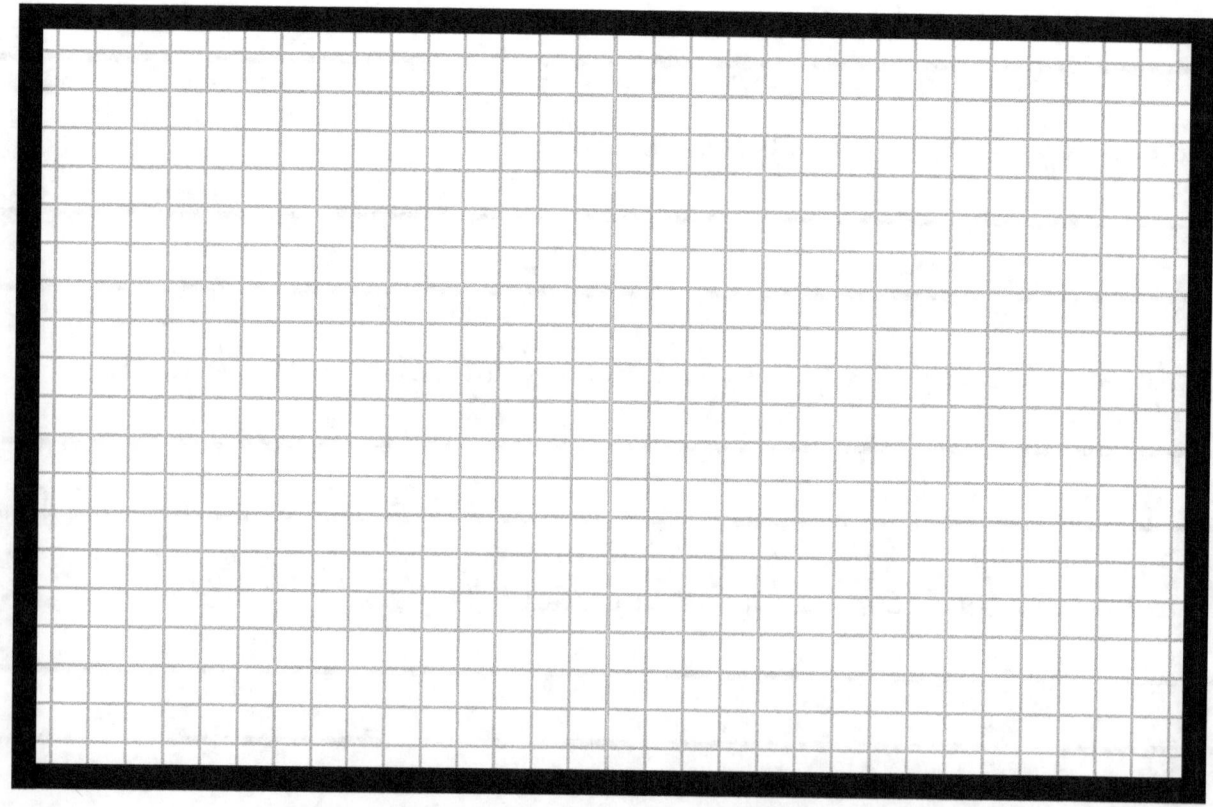

Watering Schedule   □ S   □ M   □ T   □ W   □ TH   □ F   □ S

Dates

Fertilize: | | | | | | | |

Mulch: | | | | | | | |

Prune: | | | | | | | |

Date of 1st Harvest   ___ / ___ / ___

Type of Fertilizer/Compost   _____

Pest Control   _____

Pruning Notes   _____

_____

Success of Crop/Quantity Harvested

_____

_____

Notes Regarding Success of Planting/Suggestions for Next Year

_____

_____

Unique Challenges This Growing Season (Heat/Frost/Pests)

_____

_____

Seed/Plant Variety _____

Seeds ☐ OR Starts ☐

Seed Supplier/
  Place of Purchase _____

Date Seeds Started __ / __ / __

Quantity Planted _____

Date Starts Planted in Garden __ / __ / __

Intercropping With _____

Garden Bed Layout/Sketch of Planting & Intercropping

Bed # _____

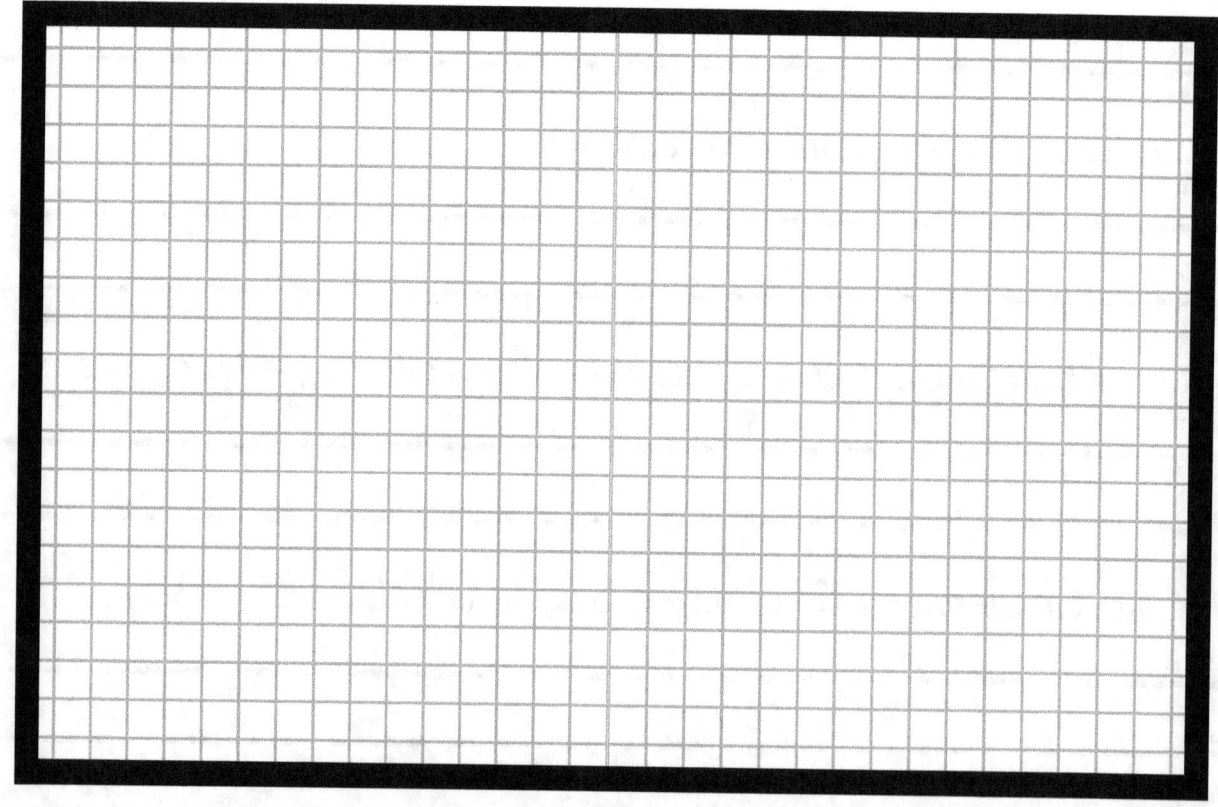

Watering Schedule | S | M | T | W | TH | F | S |

Dates

Fertilize:

Mulch:

Prune:

Date of 1st Harvest ___ / ___ / ___

Type of Fertilizer/Compost _____

Pest Control _____

Pruning Notes _____

_____

Success of Crop/Quantity Harvested

_____

_____

Notes Regarding Success of Planting/Suggestions for Next Year

_____

_____

Unique Challenges This Growing Season (Heat/Frost/Pests)

_____

_____

Seed/Plant Variety _____

Seeds ☐   OR   Starts ☐

Seed Supplier/

Place of Purchase _____

Date Seeds Started   __ / __ / __

Quantity Planted _____

Date Starts Planted in Garden   __ / __ / __

Intercropping With _____

Garden Bed Layout/Sketch of Planting & Intercropping

Bed # _____

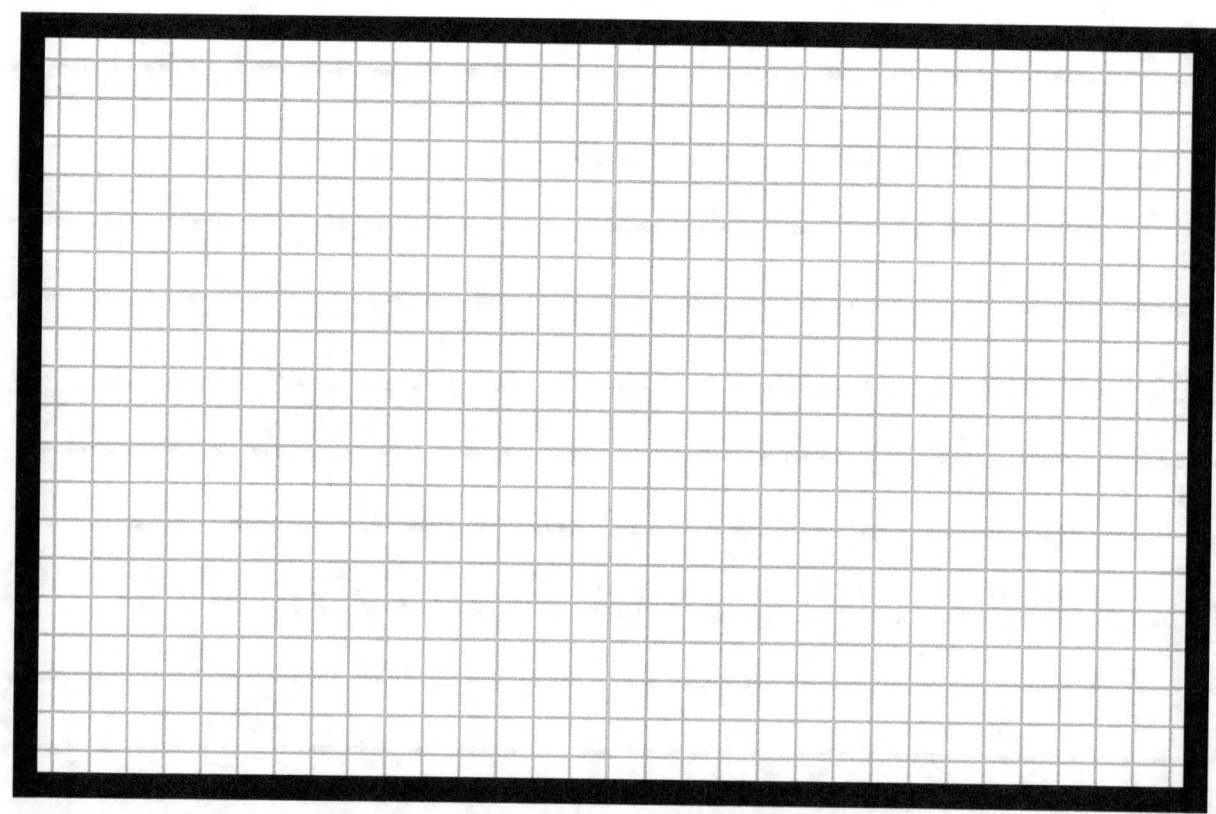

Watering Schedule | S | M | T | W | TH | F | S |

Dates

Fertilize: | | | | | | | | |
| --- | --- | --- | --- | --- | --- | --- | --- |
| | | | | | | | |

Mulch: | | | | | | | | |
| --- | --- | --- | --- | --- | --- | --- | --- |
| | | | | | | | |

Prune: | | | | | | | | |
| --- | --- | --- | --- | --- | --- | --- | --- |
| | | | | | | | |

Date of 1st Harvest   —— / —— / ——

Type of Fertilizer/Compost _____

Pest Control _____

Pruning Notes _____

_____

Success of Crop/Quantity Harvested

_____

_____

Notes Regarding Success of Planting/Suggestions for Next Year

_____

_____

Unique Challenges This Growing Season (Heat/Frost/Pests)

_____

_____

Seed/Plant Variety _____

Seeds ☐   OR   Starts ☐

Seed Supplier/
  Place of Purchase _____

Date Seeds Started   __ / __ / __

Quantity Planted _____

Date Starts Planted in Garden   __ / __ / __

Intercropping With _____

Garden Bed Layout/Sketch of Planting & Intercropping

Bed # _____

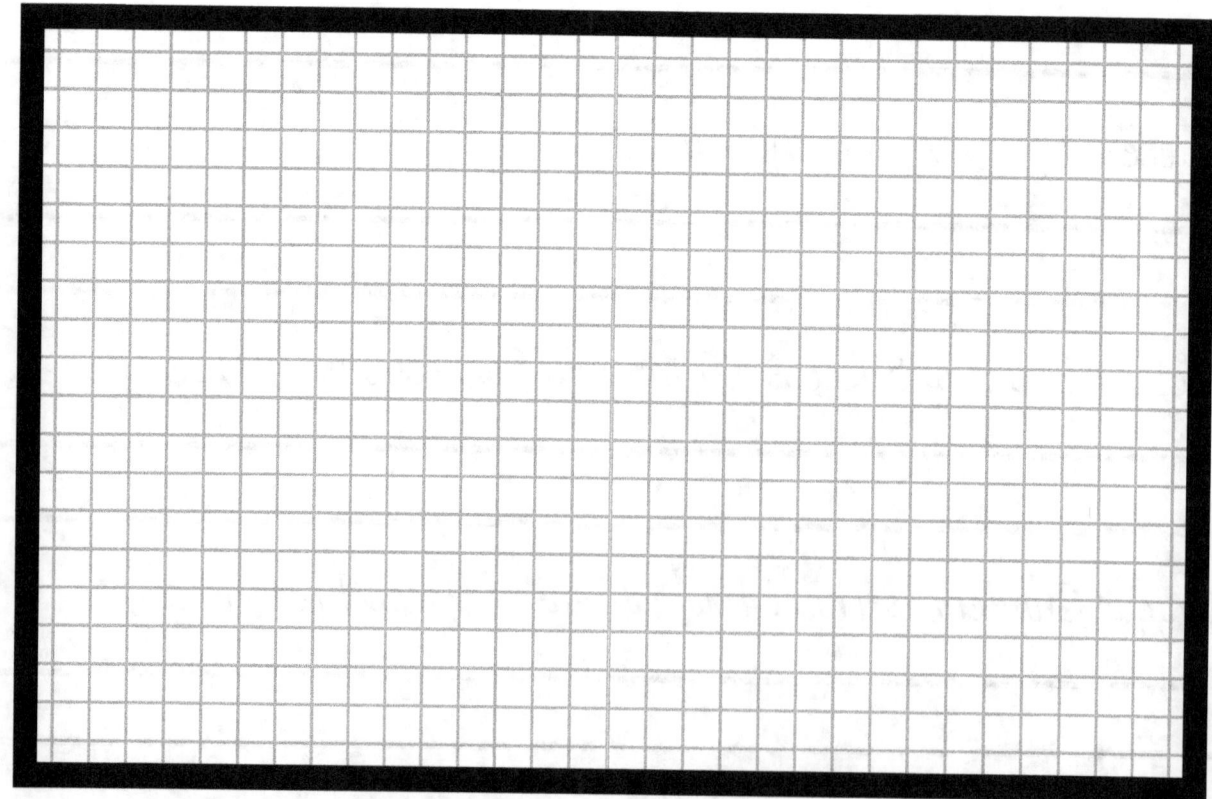

Watering Schedule S M T W TH F S

Dates

Fertilize: | | | | | | | |
|---|---|---|---|---|---|---|

Mulch: | | | | | | | |
|---|---|---|---|---|---|---|

Prune: | | | | | | | |
|---|---|---|---|---|---|---|

Date of 1st Harvest   —— / —— / ——

Type of Fertilizer/Compost _____

Pest Control _____

Pruning Notes _____

_____

Success of Crop/Quantity Harvested

_____

_____

Notes Regarding Success of Planting/Suggestions for Next Year

_____

_____

Unique Challenges This Growing Season (Heat/Frost/Pests)

_____

_____

Seed/Plant Variety _____

Seeds ☐   OR   Starts ☐

Seed Supplier/
  Place of Purchase _____

Date Seeds Started ___/___/___

Quantity Planted _____

Date Starts Planted in Garden ___/___/___

Intercropping With _____

Garden Bed Layout/Sketch of Planting & Intercropping
Bed # _____

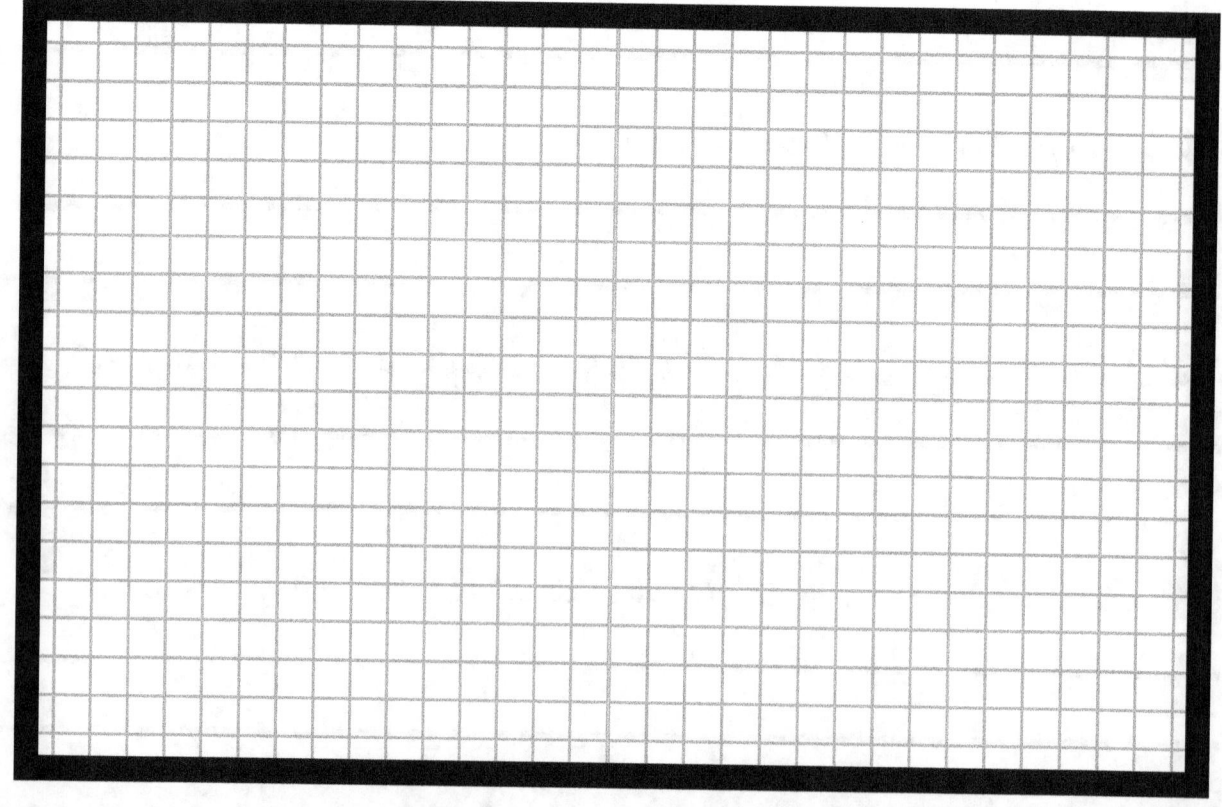

Watering Schedule   S   M   T   W   TH   F   S

Dates

Fertilize:

Mulch:

Prune:

Date of 1st Harvest   ___ / ___ / ___

Type of Fertilizer/Compost   _____

Pest Control   _____

Pruning Notes   _____

_____

Success of Crop/Quantity Harvested

_____

_____

Notes Regarding Success of Planting/Suggestions for Next Year

_____

_____

Unique Challenges This Growing Season (Heat/Frost/Pests)

_____

_____

Seed/Plant Variety _____

Seeds ☐ OR Starts ☐

Seed Supplier/
Place of Purchase _____

Date Seeds Started ___/___/___

Quantity Planted _____

Date Starts Planted in Garden ___/___/___

Intercropping With _____

Garden Bed Layout/Sketch of Planting & Intercropping

Bed # _____

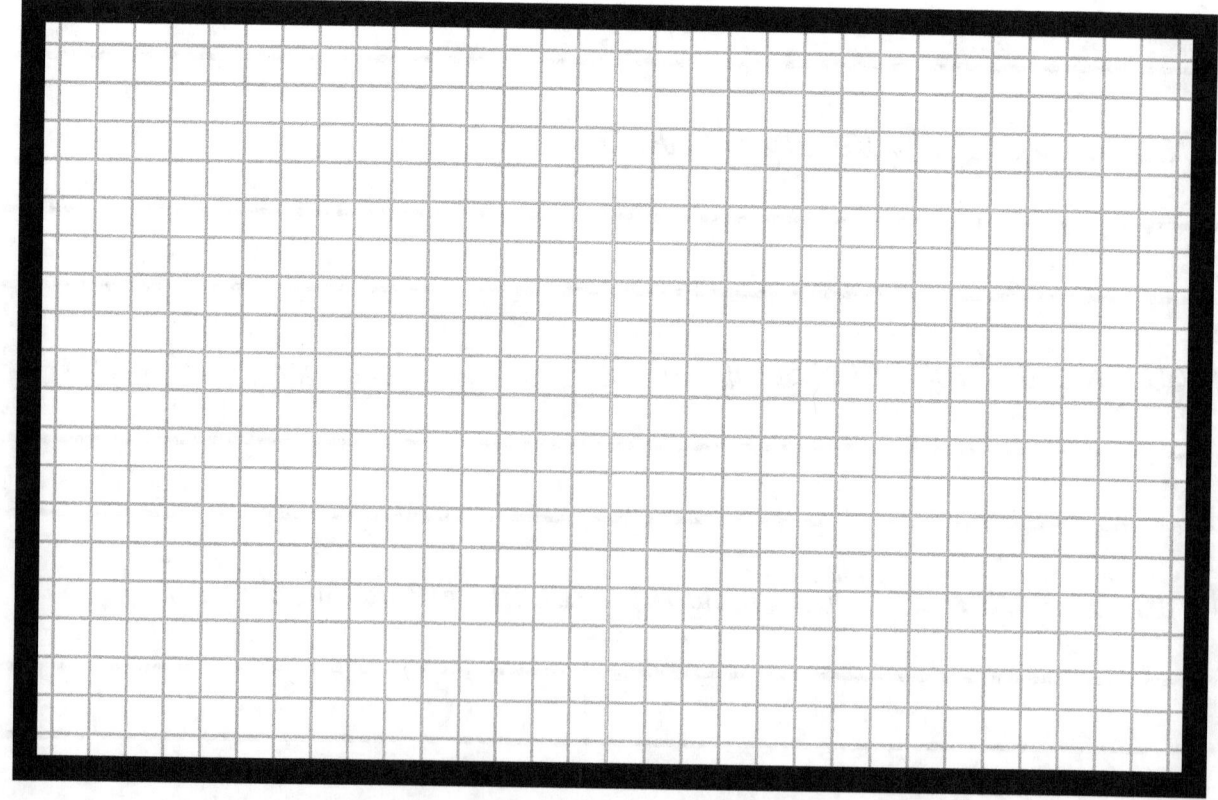

Watering Schedule | S | M | T | W | TH | F | S |

Dates

Fertilize:
| | | | | | | | |

Mulch:
| | | | | | | | |

Prune:
| | | | | | | | |

Date of 1st Harvest ___ / ___ / ___

Type of Fertilizer/Compost _____

Pest Control _____

Pruning Notes _____

_____

Success of Crop/Quantity Harvested

_____

_____

Notes Regarding Success of Planting/Suggestions for Next Year

_____

_____

Unique Challenges This Growing Season (Heat/Frost/Pests)

_____

_____

Seed/Plant Variety _____

Seeds ☐   OR   Starts ☐

Seed Supplier/
  Place of Purchase _____

Date Seeds Started   __ / __ / __

Quantity Planted _____

Date Starts Planted in Garden   __ / __ / __

Intercropping With _____

Garden Bed Layout/Sketch of Planting & Intercropping

Bed # _____

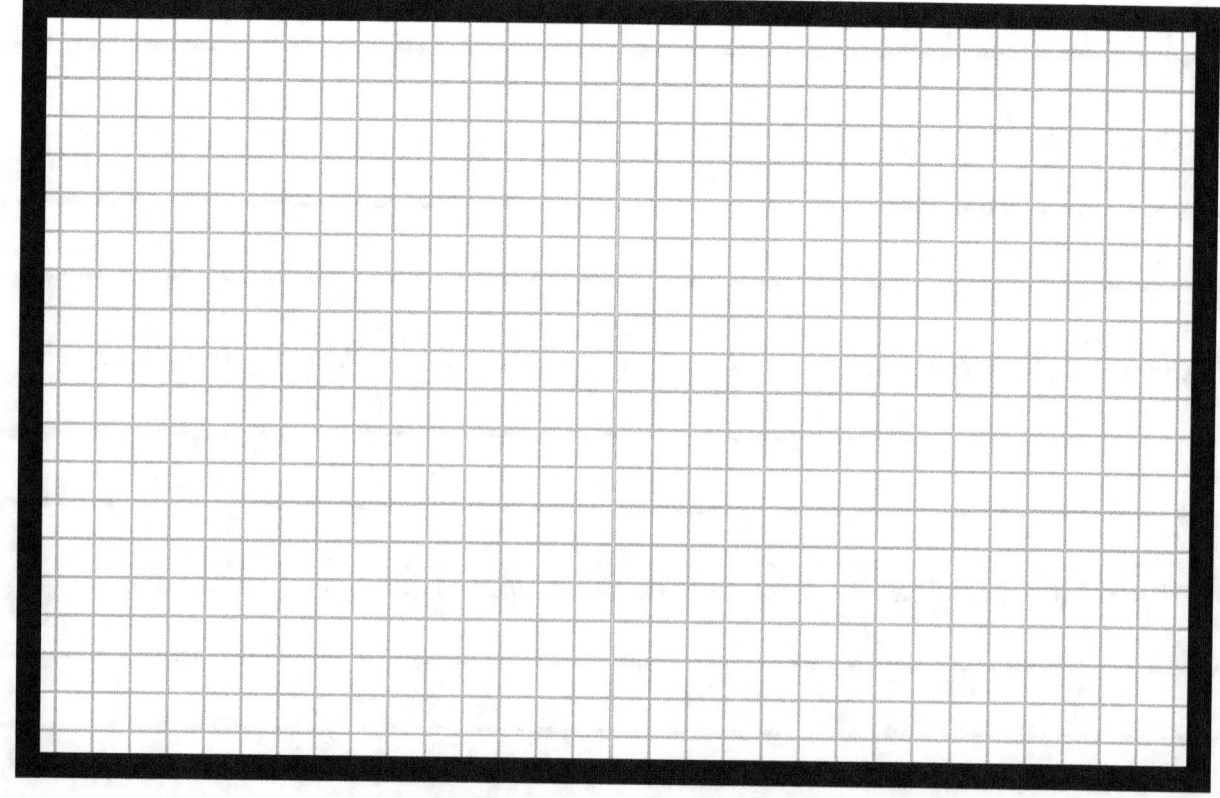

Watering Schedule ☐S ☐M ☐T ☐W ☐TH ☐F ☐S

Dates

Fertilize: ☐ ☐ ☐ ☐ ☐ ☐ ☐ ☐

Mulch: ☐ ☐ ☐ ☐ ☐ ☐ ☐ ☐

Prune: ☐ ☐ ☐ ☐ ☐ ☐ ☐ ☐

Date of 1st Harvest __ / __ / __

Type of Fertilizer/Compost _____

Pest Control _____

Pruning Notes _____

_____

Success of Crop/Quantity Harvested

_____

_____

Notes Regarding Success of Planting/Suggestions for Next Year

_____

_____

Unique Challenges This Growing Season (Heat/Frost/Pests)

_____

_____

Seed/Plant Variety _____

Seeds ☐ OR Starts ☐

Seed Supplier/
Place of Purchase _____

Date Seeds Started ___/___/___

Quantity Planted _____

Date Starts Planted in Garden ___/___/___

Intercropping With _____

Garden Bed Layout/Sketch of Planting & Intercropping

Bed # _____

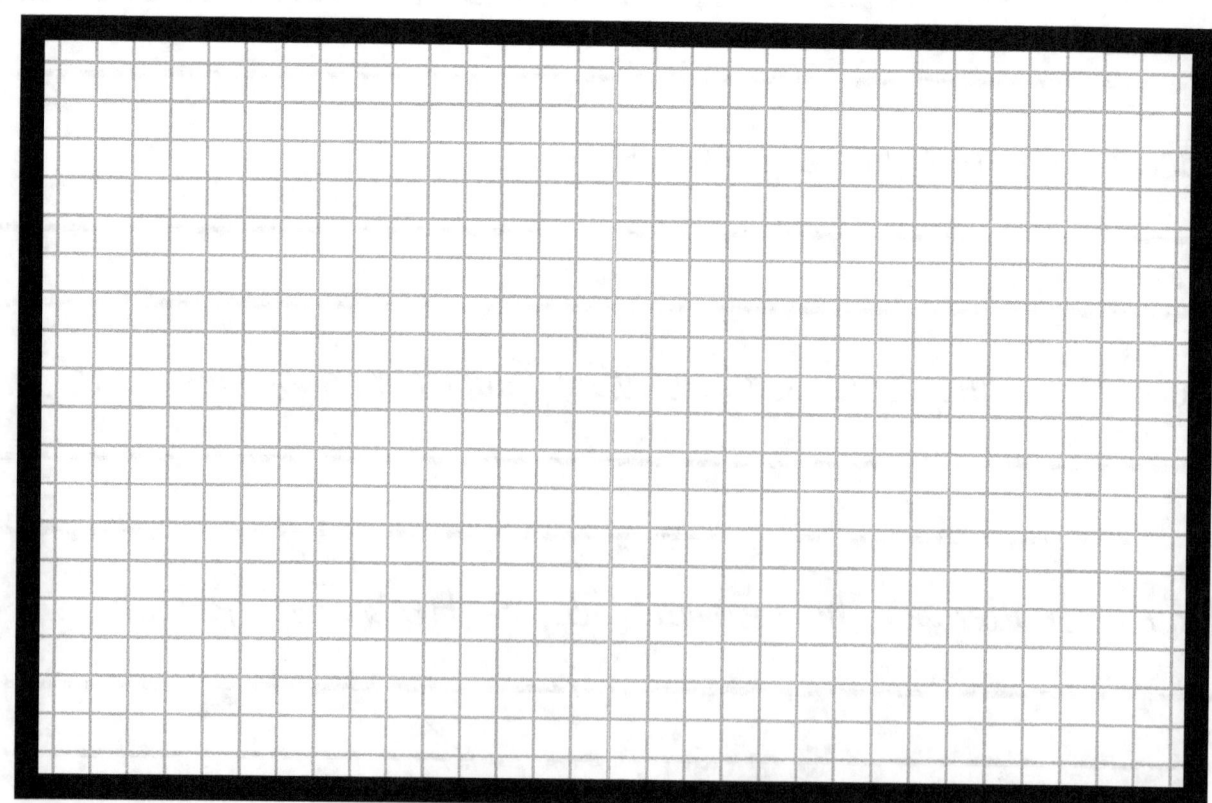

Watering Schedule | S | M | T | W | TH | F | S |

Dates

Fertilize: | | | | | | | | |

Mulch: | | | | | | | | |

Prune: | | | | | | | | |

Date of 1st Harvest   —— / —— / ——

Type of Fertilizer/Compost _____

Pest Control _____

Pruning Notes _____

_____

Success of Crop/Quantity Harvested

_____

_____

Notes Regarding Success of Planting/Suggestions for Next Year

_____

_____

Unique Challenges This Growing Season (Heat/Frost/Pests)

_____

_____

Seed/Plant Variety _____

Seeds ☐   OR   Starts ☐

Seed Supplier/
   Place of Purchase _____

Date Seeds Started   __ / __ / __

Quantity Planted _____

Date Starts Planted in Garden   __ / __ / __

Intercropping With _____

Garden Bed Layout/Sketch of Planting & Intercropping
Bed # _____

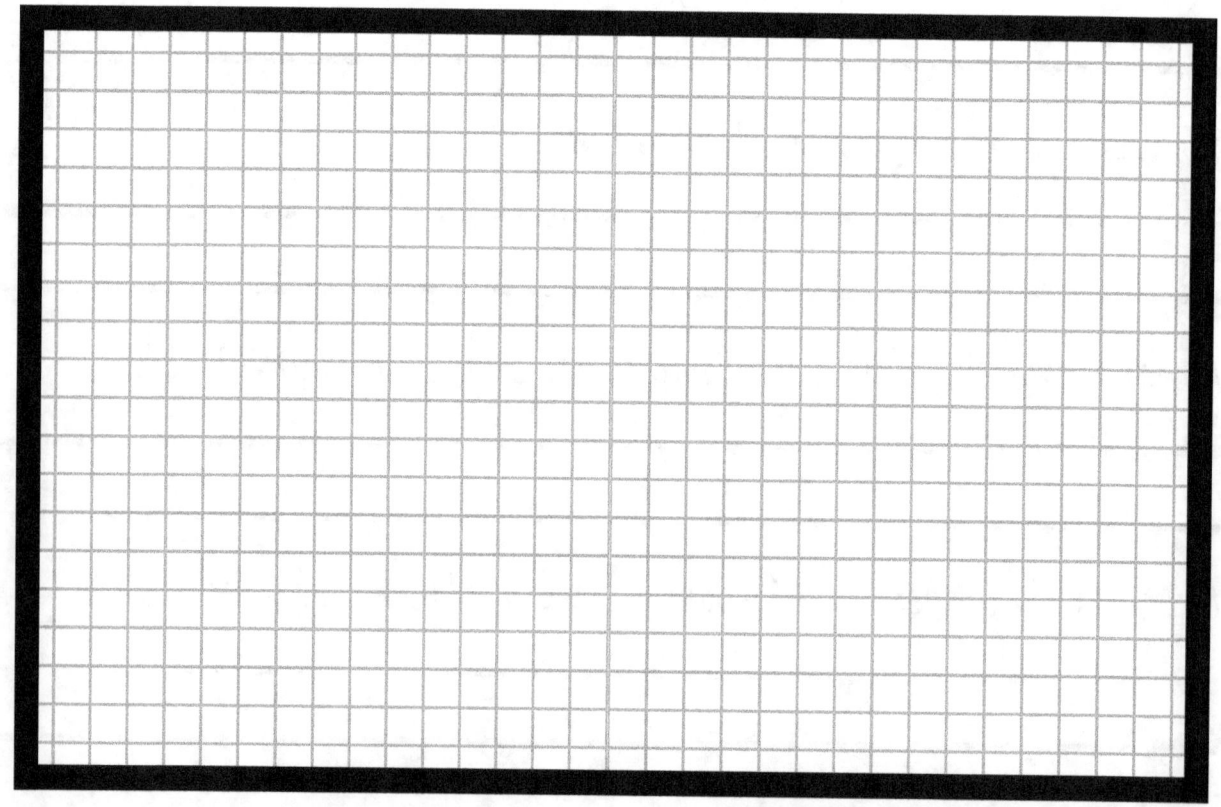

Watering Schedule   S   M   T   W   TH   F   S

Dates

Fertilize:

Mulch:

Prune:

Date of 1st Harvest   —— / —— / ——

Type of Fertilizer/Compost _____

Pest Control _____

Pruning Notes _____

_____

Success of Crop/Quantity Harvested

_____

_____

Notes Regarding Success of Planting/Suggestions for Next Year

_____

_____

Unique Challenges This Growing Season (Heat/Frost/Pests)

_____

_____

Seed/Plant Variety _____

Seeds ☐ OR Starts ☐

Seed Supplier/
  Place of Purchase _____

Date Seeds Started ___/___/___

Quantity Planted _____

Date Starts Planted in Garden ___/___/___

Intercropping With _____

Garden Bed Layout/Sketch of Planting & Intercropping
Bed #_____

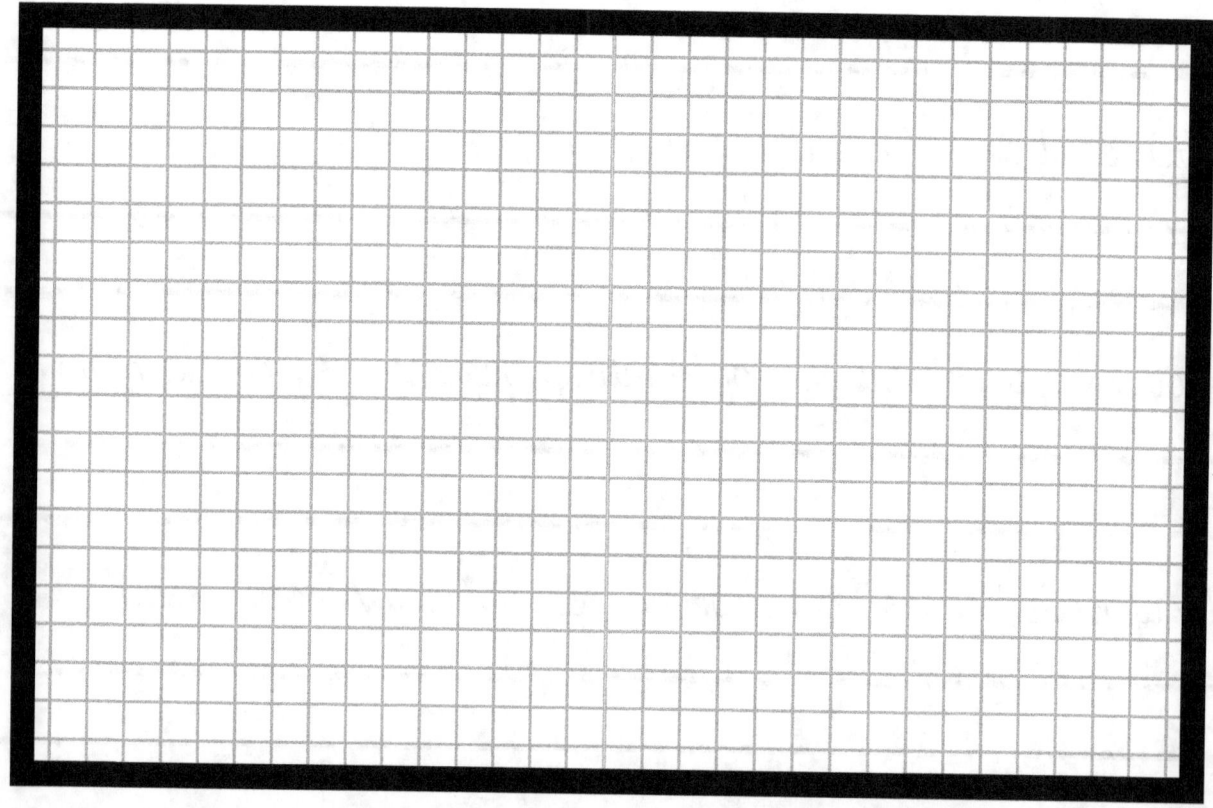

Watering Schedule | S | M | T | W | TH | F | S |

Dates

Fertilize:

Mulch:

Prune:

Date of 1st Harvest   —— / —— / ——

Type of Fertilizer/Compost   _____

Pest Control   _____

Pruning Notes   _____

_____

Success of Crop/Quantity Harvested

_____

_____

Notes Regarding Success of Planting/Suggestions for Next Year

_____

_____

Unique Challenges This Growing Season (Heat/Frost/Pests)

_____

_____

Seed/Plant Variety _____

Seeds ☐ OR Starts ☐

Seed Supplier/

Place of Purchase _____

Date Seeds Started __ / __ / __

Quantity Planted _____

Date Starts Planted in Garden __ / __ / __

Intercropping With _____

Garden Bed Layout/Sketch of Planting & Intercropping

Bed # _____

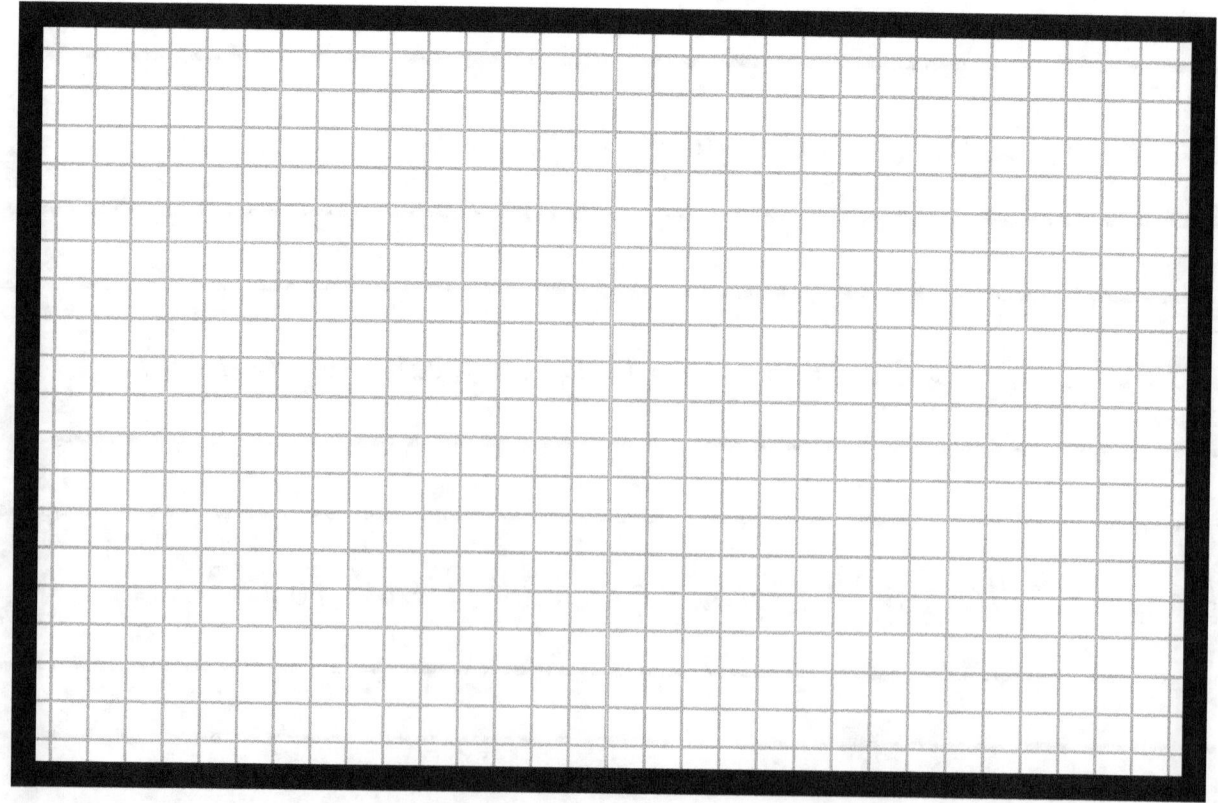

Watering Schedule   S   M   T   W   TH   F   S

Dates

Fertilize:

Mulch:

Prune:

Date of 1st Harvest   — / — / —

Type of Fertilizer/Compost _____

Pest Control _____

Pruning Notes _____

_____

Success of Crop/Quantity Harvested

_____

_____

Notes Regarding Success of Planting/Suggestions for Next Year

_____

_____

Unique Challenges This Growing Season (Heat/Frost/Pests)

_____

_____

Seed/Plant Variety _____

Seeds ☐ OR Starts ☐

Seed Supplier/
  Place of Purchase _____

Date Seeds Started ___ / ___ / ___

Quantity Planted _____

Date Starts Planted in Garden ___ / ___ / ___

Intercropping With _____

Garden Bed Layout/Sketch of Planting & Intercropping

Bed # _____

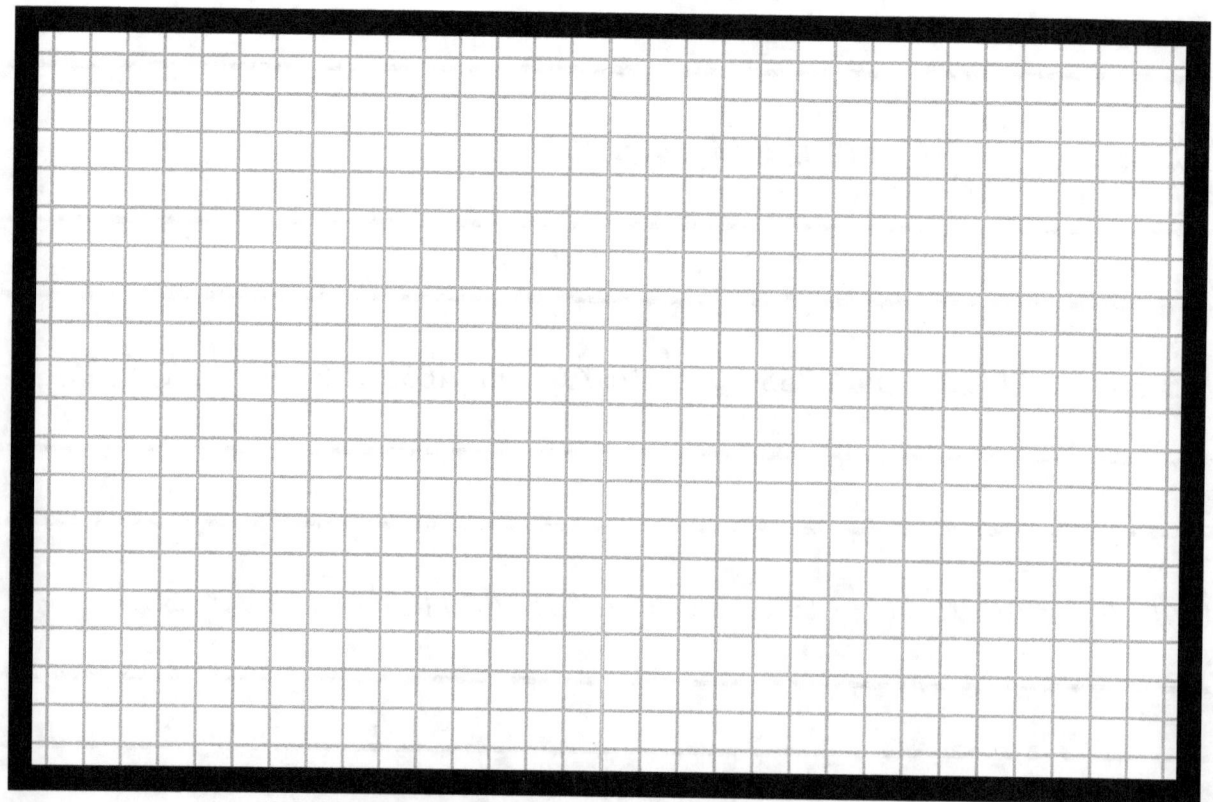

Watering Schedule   S   M   T   W   TH   F   S

Dates

Fertilize:

Mulch:

Prune:

Date of 1st Harvest   __ / __ / __

Type of Fertilizer/Compost _____

Pest Control _____

Pruning Notes _____

_____

Success of Crop/Quantity Harvested

_____

_____

Notes Regarding Success of Planting/Suggestions for Next Year

_____

_____

Unique Challenges This Growing Season (Heat/Frost/Pests)

_____

_____

Seed/Plant Variety _____

Seeds ☐   OR   Starts ☐

Seed Supplier/
  Place of Purchase _____

Date Seeds Started ___ / ___ / ___

Quantity Planted _____

Date Starts Planted in Garden ___ / ___ / ___

Intercropping With _____

Garden Bed Layout/Sketch of Planting & Intercropping
Bed # _____

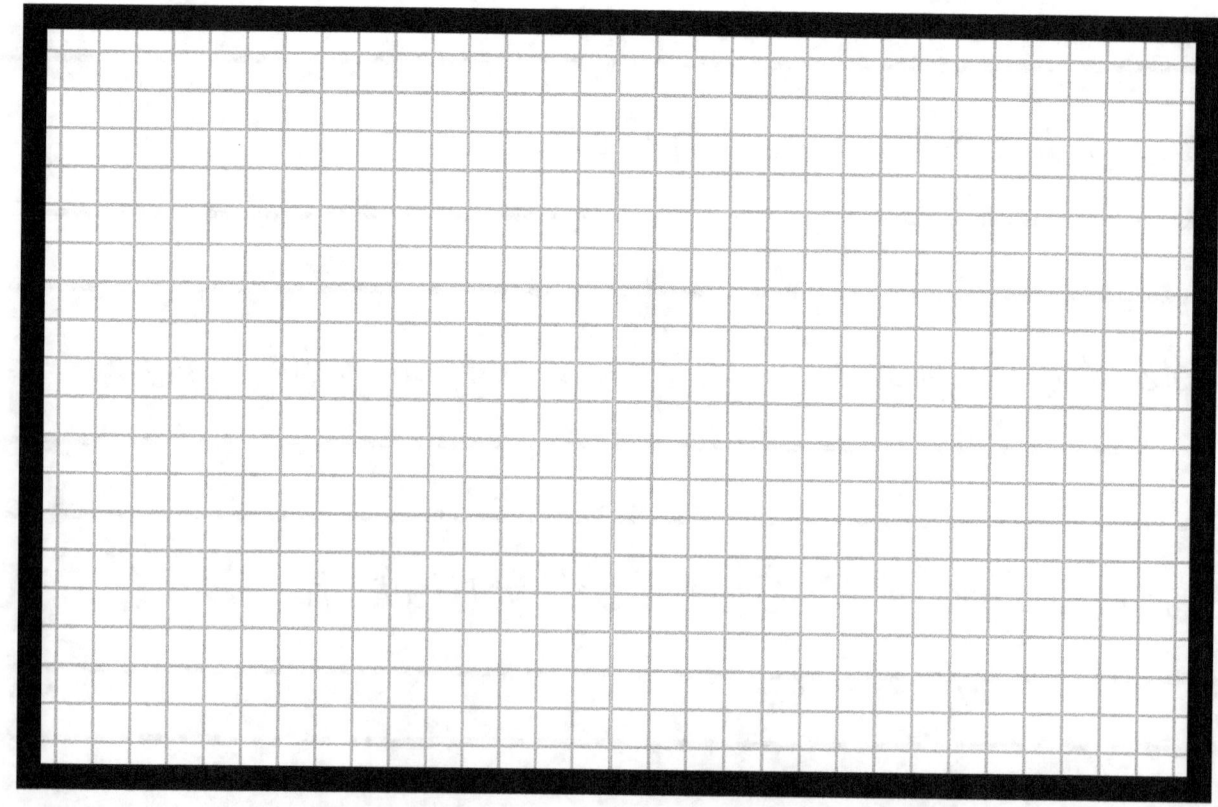

Watering Schedule   ☐ S   ☐ M   ☐ T   ☐ W   ☐ TH   ☐ F   ☐ S

Dates

Fertilize: | | | | | | | | |

Mulch: | | | | | | | | |

Prune: | | | | | | | | |

Date of 1st Harvest   __ / __ / __

Type of Fertilizer/Compost _____

Pest Control _____

Pruning Notes _____

_____

Success of Crop/Quantity Harvested

_____

_____

Notes Regarding Success of Planting/Suggestions for Next Year

_____

_____

Unique Challenges This Growing Season (Heat/Frost/Pests)

_____

_____

Seed/Plant Variety _____

Seeds ☐ OR Starts ☐

Seed Supplier/
  Place of Purchase _____

Date Seeds Started __ / __ / __

Quantity Planted _____

Date Starts Planted in Garden __ / __ / __

Intercropping With _____

Garden Bed Layout/Sketch of Planting & Intercropping

Bed # _____

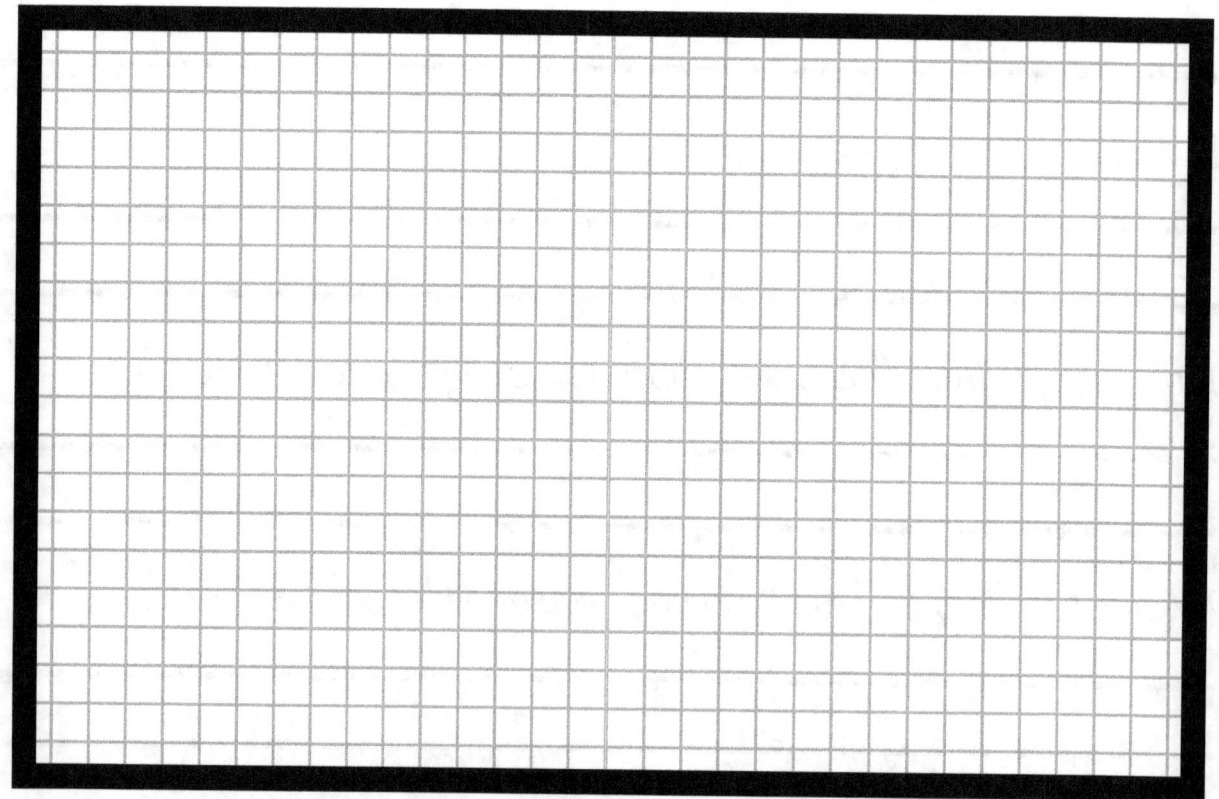

Watering Schedule | S | M | T | W | TH | F | S |

Dates

Fertilize:

| | | | | | | | |

Mulch:

| | | | | | | | |

Prune:

| | | | | | | | |

Date of 1st Harvest   __ / __ / __

Type of Fertilizer/Compost _____

Pest Control _____

Pruning Notes _____

_____

Success of Crop/Quantity Harvested

_____

_____

Notes Regarding Success of Planting/Suggestions for Next Year

_____

_____

Unique Challenges This Growing Season (Heat/Frost/Pests)

_____

_____

Seed/Plant Variety _____

Seeds ☐   OR   Starts ☐

Seed Supplier/
Place of Purchase _____

Date Seeds Started ___ / ___ / ___

Quantity Planted _____

Date Starts Planted in Garden ___ / ___ / ___

Intercropping With _____

Garden Bed Layout/Sketch of Planting & Intercropping

Bed # _____

Watering Schedule   S   M   T   W   TH   F   S

Dates

Fertilize:							

Mulch:							

Prune:							

Date of 1st Harvest   ___ / ___ / ___

Type of Fertilizer/Compost   _____

Pest Control   _____

Pruning Notes   _____

_____

Success of Crop/Quantity Harvested

_____

_____

Notes Regarding Success of Planting/Suggestions for Next Year

_____

_____

Unique Challenges This Growing Season (Heat/Frost/Pests)

_____

_____

Seed/Plant Variety _____

Seeds ☐　OR　Starts ☐

Seed Supplier/
Place of Purchase　_____

Date Seeds Started　__/__/__

Quantity Planted　_____

Date Starts Planted in Garden　__/__/__

Intercropping With　_____

Garden Bed Layout/Sketch of Planting & Intercropping

Bed # _____

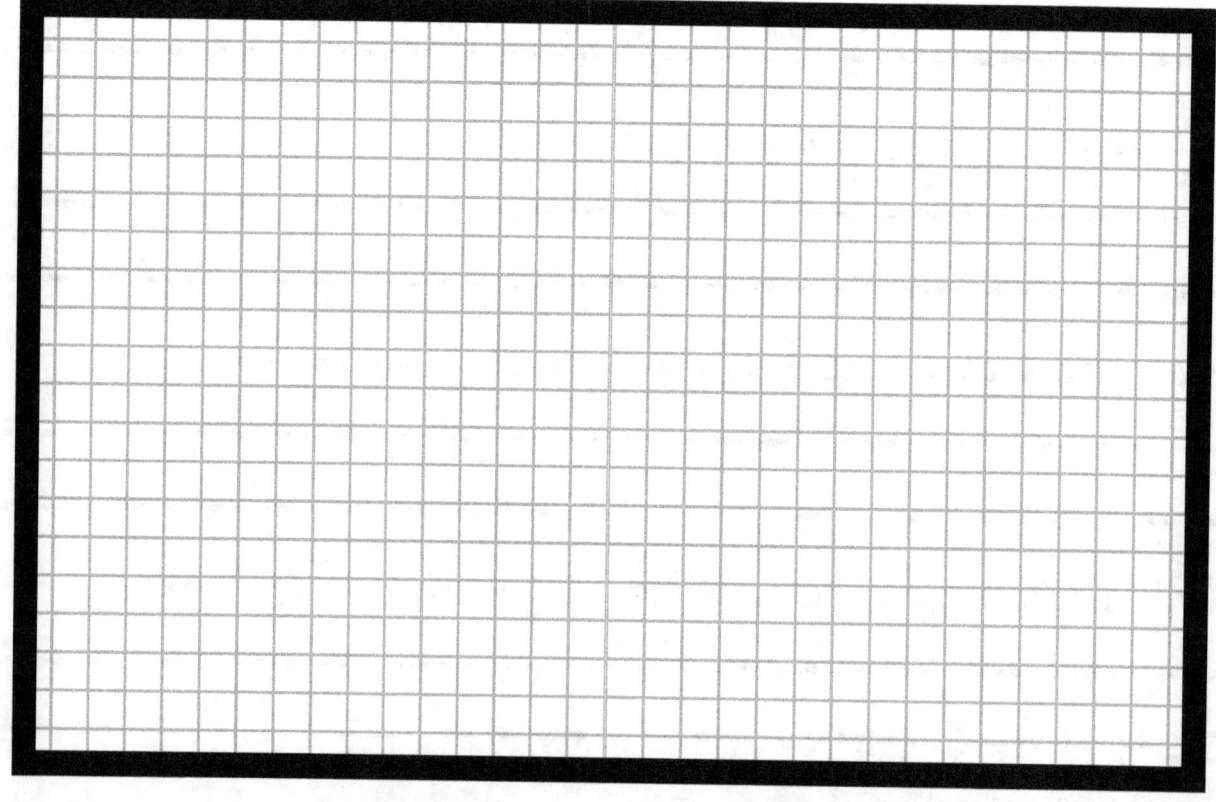

Watering Schedule   □ S   □ M   □ T   □ W   □ TH   □ F   □ S

Dates

Fertilize:

Mulch:

Prune:

Date of 1st Harvest   __ / __ / __

Type of Fertilizer/Compost _____

Pest Control _____

Pruning Notes _____

_____

Success of Crop/Quantity Harvested

_____

_____

Notes Regarding Success of Planting/Suggestions for Next Year

_____

_____

Unique Challenges This Growing Season (Heat/Frost/Pests)

_____

_____

Seed/Plant Variety _____

Seeds ☐ OR Starts ☐

Seed Supplier/
  Place of Purchase _____

Date Seeds Started ___/___/___

Quantity Planted _____

Date Starts Planted in Garden ___/___/___

Intercropping With _____

Garden Bed Layout/Sketch of Planting & Intercropping

Bed # _____

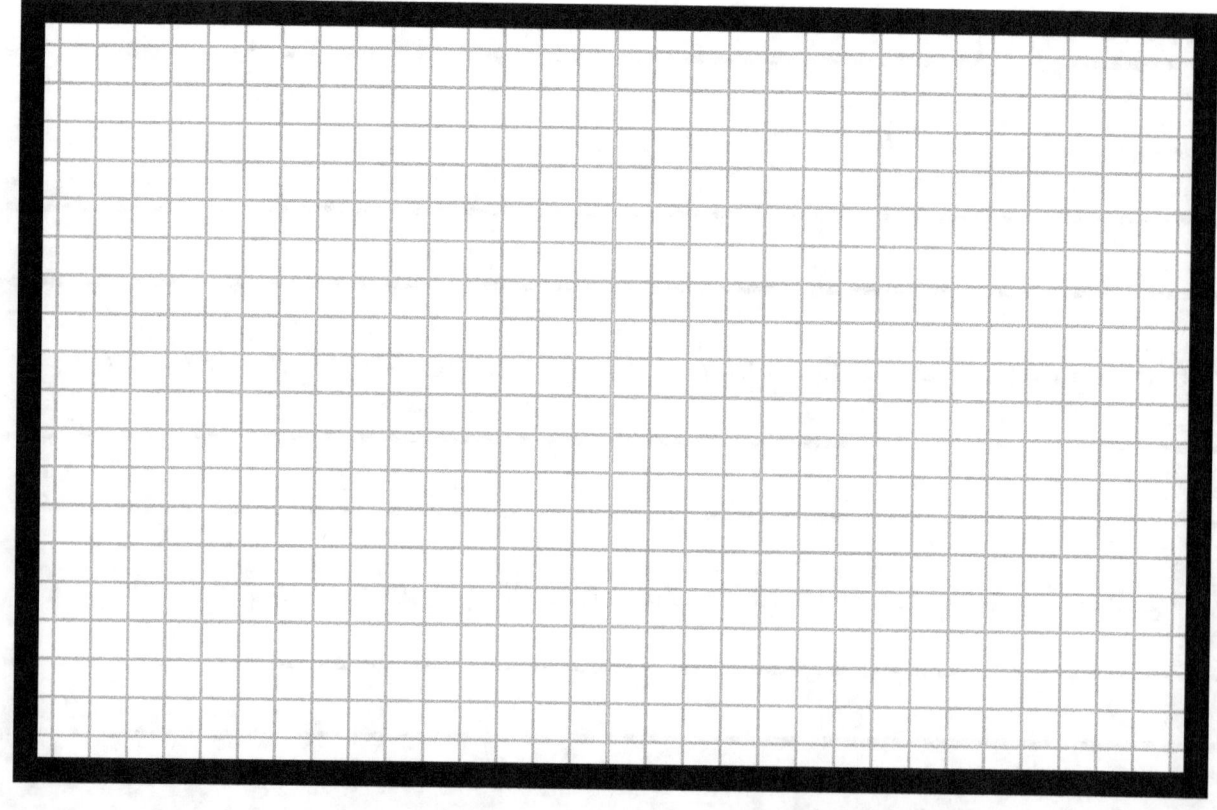

Watering Schedule   [S]   [M]   [T]   [W]   [TH]   [F]   [S]

Dates

Fertilize:

Mulch:

Prune:

Date of 1st Harvest   —— / —— / ——

Type of Fertilizer/Compost _____

Pest Control _____

Pruning Notes _____

_____

Success of Crop/Quantity Harvested

_____

_____

Notes Regarding Success of Planting/Suggestions for Next Year

_____

_____

Unique Challenges This Growing Season (Heat/Frost/Pests)

_____

_____

Seed/Plant Variety _____

Seeds ☐   OR   Starts ☐

Seed Supplier/
  Place of Purchase _____

Date Seeds Started ___ / ___ / ___

Quantity Planted _____

Date Starts Planted in Garden ___ / ___ / ___

Intercropping With _____

Garden Bed Layout/Sketch of Planting & Intercropping

Bed # _____

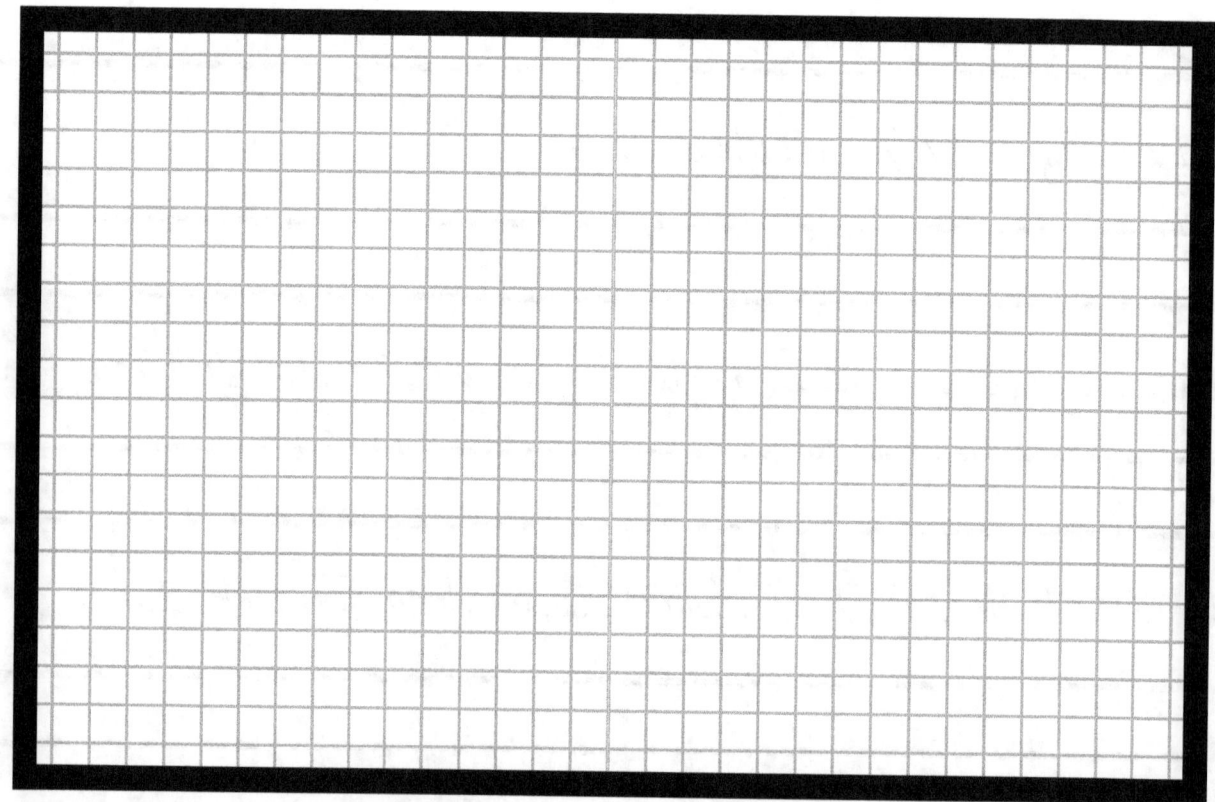

Watering Schedule   S   M   T   W   TH   F   S

Dates

Fertilize:							

Mulch:							

Prune:							

Date of 1st Harvest   __ / __ / __

Type of Fertilizer/Compost   _____

Pest Control   _____

Pruning Notes   _____

_____

Success of Crop/Quantity Harvested

_____

_____

Notes Regarding Success of Planting/Suggestions for Next Year

_____

_____

Unique Challenges This Growing Season (Heat/Frost/Pests)

_____

_____

Seed/Plant Variety _____

Seeds ☐   OR   Starts ☐

Seed Supplier/
  Place of Purchase _____

Date Seeds Started ___ / ___ / ___

Quantity Planted _____

Date Starts Planted in Garden ___ / ___ / ___

Intercropping With _____

Garden Bed Layout/Sketch of Planting & Intercropping

Bed # _____

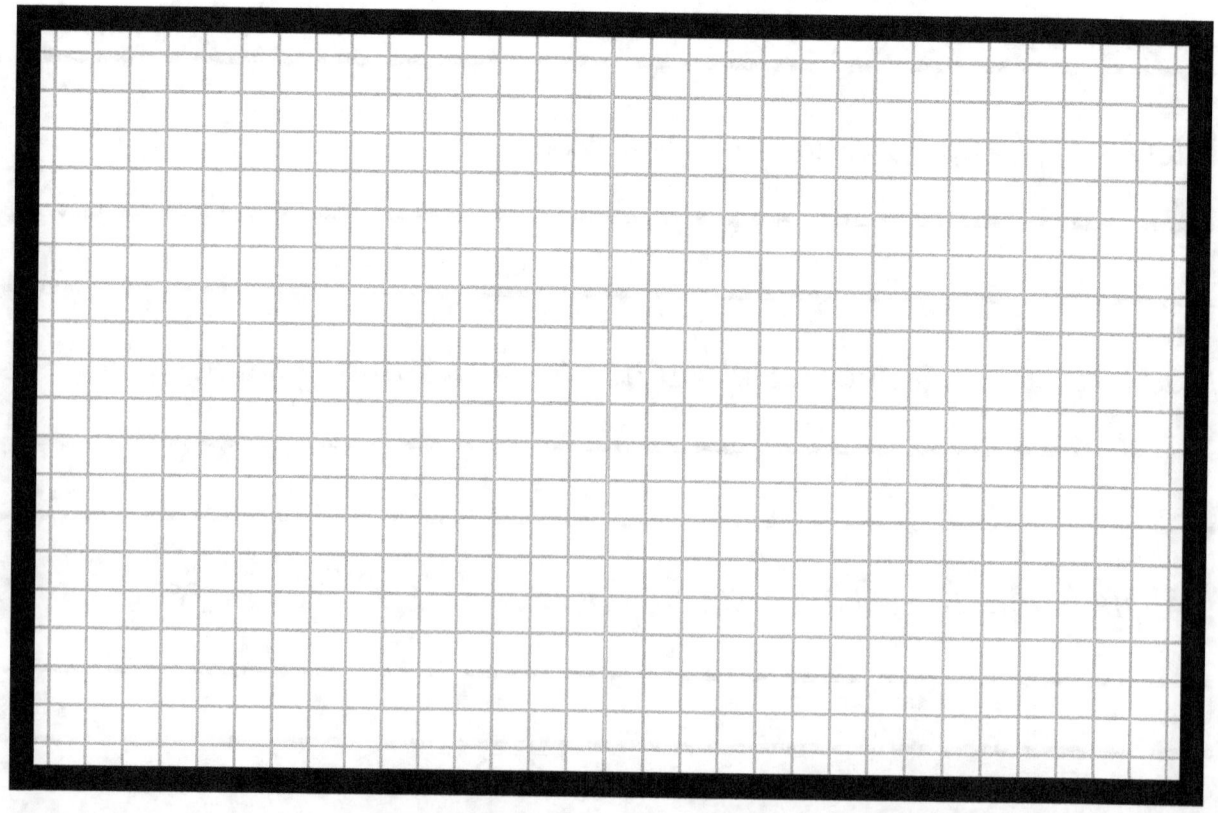

Watering Schedule | S | M | T | W | TH | F | S |

Dates

Fertilize: | | | | | | | | |

Mulch: | | | | | | | | |

Prune: | | | | | | | | |

Date of 1st Harvest ___ / ___ / ___

Type of Fertilizer/Compost _____

Pest Control _____

Pruning Notes _____

_____

Success of Crop/Quantity Harvested

_____

_____

Notes Regarding Success of Planting/Suggestions for Next Year

_____

_____

Unique Challenges This Growing Season (Heat/Frost/Pests)

_____

_____

Seed/Plant Variety _____

Seeds ☐ OR Starts ☐

Seed Supplier/
Place of Purchase _____

Date Seeds Started ___ / ___ / ___

Quantity Planted _____

Date Starts Planted in Garden ___ / ___ / ___

Intercropping With _____

Garden Bed Layout/Sketch of Planting & Intercropping

Bed # _____

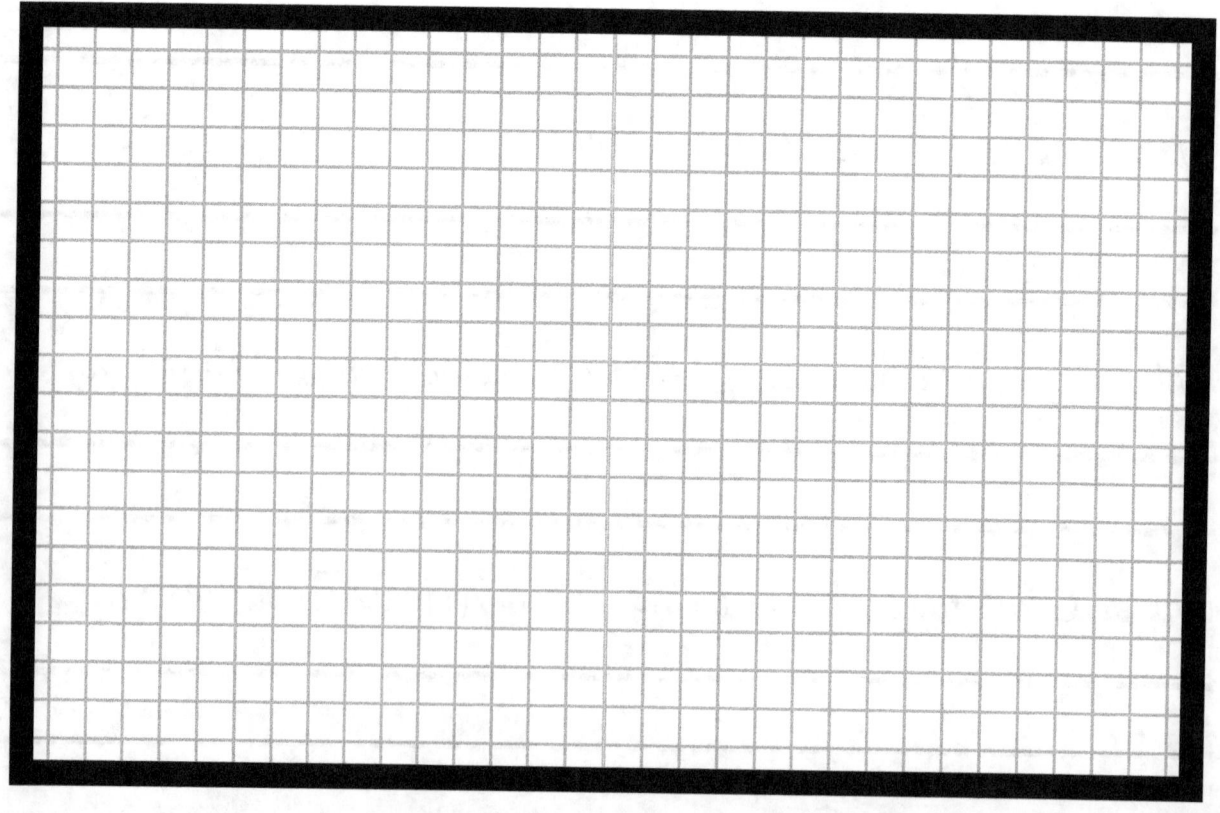

Watering Schedule | S | M | T | W | TH | F | S |

Dates

Fertilize:

Mulch:

Prune:

Date of 1st Harvest   __ / __ / __

Type of Fertilizer/Compost _____

Pest Control _____

Pruning Notes _____

_____

Success of Crop/Quantity Harvested

_____

_____

Notes Regarding Success of Planting/Suggestions for Next Year

_____

_____

Unique Challenges This Growing Season (Heat/Frost/Pests)

_____

_____

Seed/Plant Variety _____

Seeds ☐   OR   Starts ☐

Seed Supplier/
Place of Purchase _____

Date Seeds Started   __ / __ / __

Quantity Planted _____

Date Starts Planted in Garden   __ / __ / __

Intercropping With _____

Garden Bed Layout/Sketch of Planting & Intercropping

Bed # _____

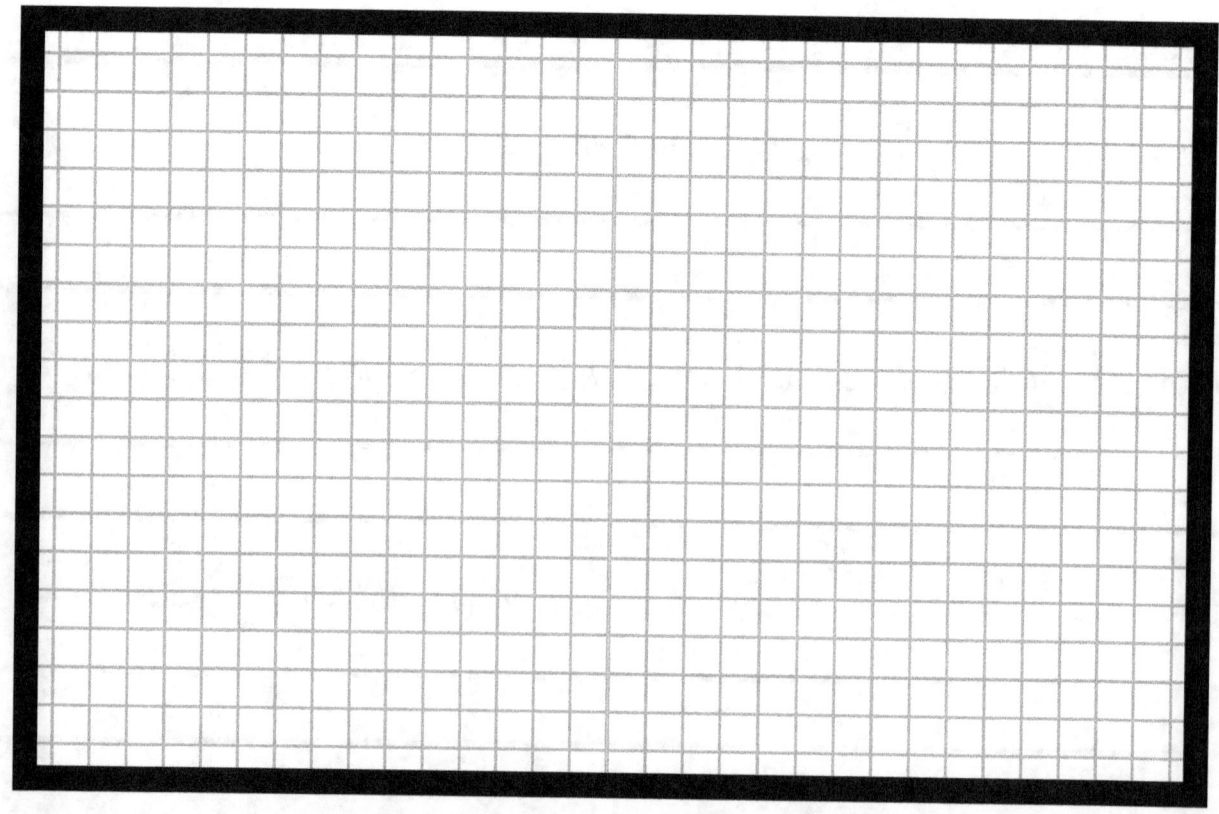

Watering Schedule | S | M | T | W | TH | F | S |

Dates

Fertilize: | | | | | | | | |

Mulch: | | | | | | | | |

Prune: | | | | | | | | |

Date of 1st Harvest — / — / —

Type of Fertilizer/Compost _____

Pest Control _____

Pruning Notes _____

_____

Success of Crop/Quantity Harvested

_____

_____

Notes Regarding Success of Planting/Suggestions for Next Year

_____

_____

Unique Challenges This Growing Season (Heat/Frost/Pests)

_____

_____

Seed/Plant Variety _____

Seeds ☐   OR   Starts ☐

Seed Supplier/
   Place of Purchase _____

Date Seeds Started ___/___/___

Quantity Planted _____

Date Starts Planted in Garden ___/___/___

Intercropping With _____

Garden Bed Layout/Sketch of Planting & Intercropping

Bed # _____

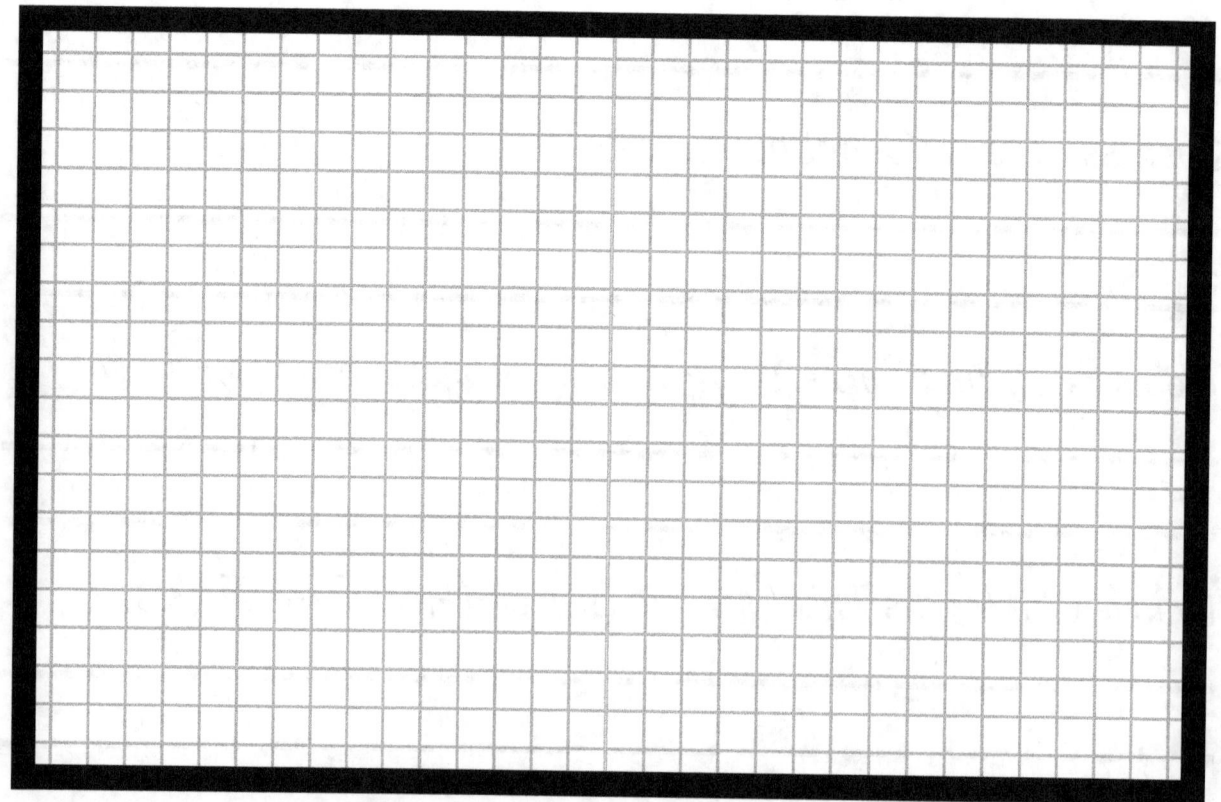

Watering Schedule   [S] [M] [T] [W] [TH] [F] [S]

Dates

Fertilize: | | | | | | | |
|---|---|---|---|---|---|---|
| | | | | | | |

Mulch: | | | | | | | |
|---|---|---|---|---|---|---|
| | | | | | | |

Prune: | | | | | | | |
|---|---|---|---|---|---|---|
| | | | | | | |

Date of 1st Harvest   __ / __ / __

Type of Fertilizer/Compost _____

Pest Control _____

Pruning Notes _____

_____

Success of Crop/Quantity Harvested

_____

_____

Notes Regarding Success of Planting/Suggestions for Next Year

_____

_____

Unique Challenges This Growing Season (Heat/Frost/Pests)

_____

_____

Seed/Plant Variety _____

Seeds ☐ OR Starts ☐

Seed Supplier/
  Place of Purchase _____

Date Seeds Started   __ / __ / __

Quantity Planted _____

Date Starts Planted in Garden   __ / __ / __

Intercropping With _____

Garden Bed Layout/Sketch of Planting & Intercropping
Bed # _____

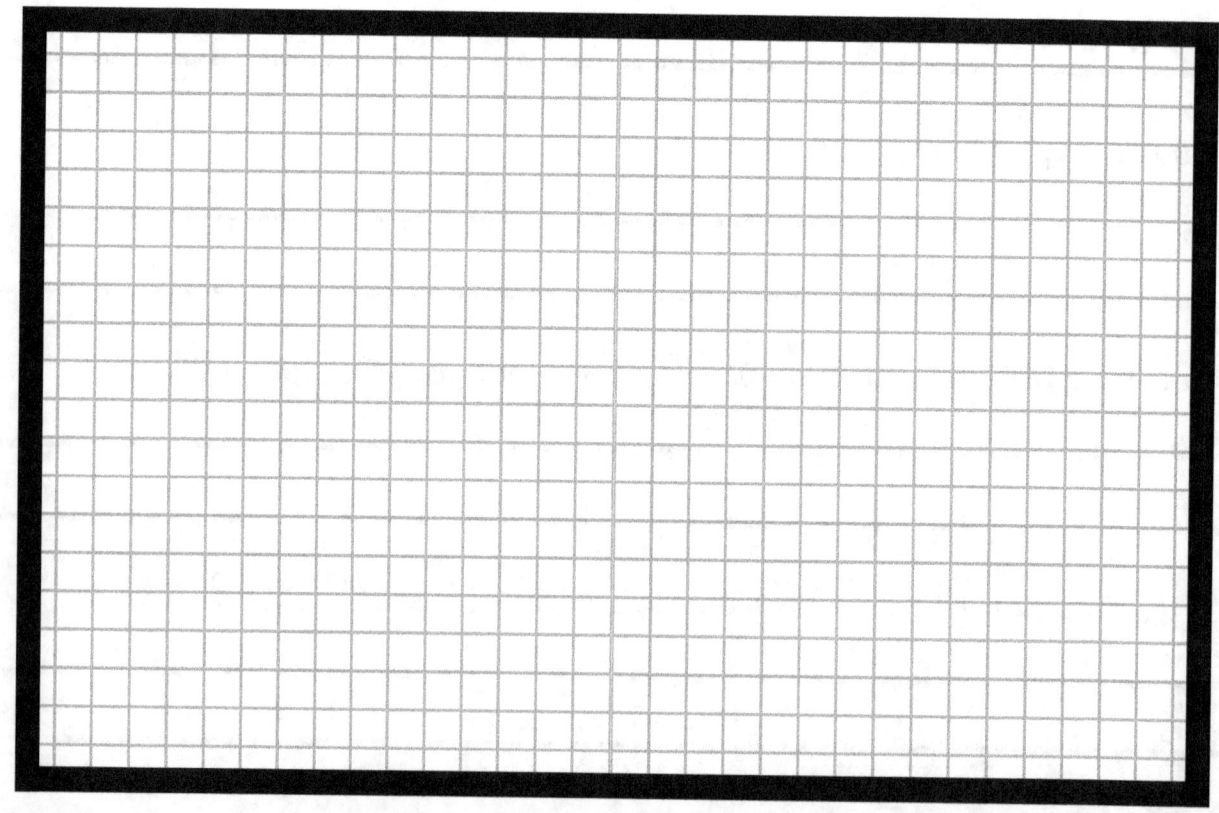

Watering Schedule   S M T W TH F S

Dates

Fertilize: | | | | | | | | |

Mulch: | | | | | | | | |

Prune: | | | | | | | | |

Date of 1st Harvest   __ / __ / __

Type of Fertilizer/Compost _____

Pest Control _____

Pruning Notes _____

_____

Success of Crop/Quantity Harvested

_____

_____

Notes Regarding Success of Planting/Suggestions for Next Year

_____

_____

Unique Challenges This Growing Season (Heat/Frost/Pests)

_____

_____

Seed/Plant Variety _____

Seeds ☐   OR   Starts ☐

Seed Supplier/
Place of Purchase _____

Date Seeds Started   __ / __ / __

Quantity Planted _____

Date Starts Planted in Garden   __ / __ / __

Intercropping With _____

Garden Bed Layout/Sketch of Planting & Intercropping
Bed # _____

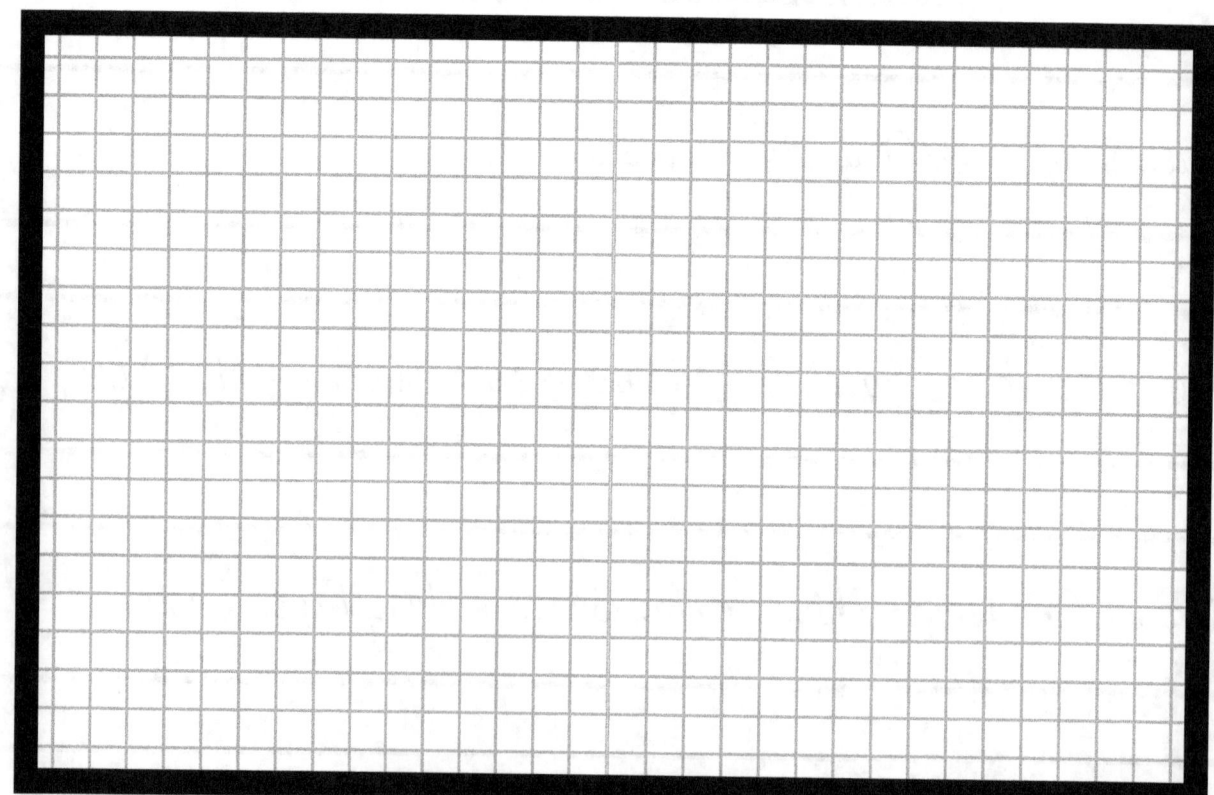

Watering Schedule   S M T W TH F S

Dates

Fertilize: ☐ ☐ ☐ ☐ ☐ ☐ ☐ ☐

Mulch: ☐ ☐ ☐ ☐ ☐ ☐ ☐ ☐

Prune: ☐ ☐ ☐ ☐ ☐ ☐ ☐ ☐

Date of 1st Harvest ___ / ___ / ___

Type of Fertilizer/Compost _____

Pest Control _____

Pruning Notes _____

_____

Success of Crop/Quantity Harvested

_____

_____

Notes Regarding Success of Planting/Suggestions for Next Year

_____

_____

Unique Challenges This Growing Season (Heat/Frost/Pests)

_____

_____

Seed/Plant Variety _____

Seeds ☐   OR   Starts ☐

Seed Supplier/
   Place of Purchase   _____

Date Seeds Started   __ / __ / __

Quantity Planted   _____

Date Starts Planted in Garden   __ / __ / __

Intercropping With   _____

Garden Bed Layout/Sketch of Planting & Intercropping

Bed # _____

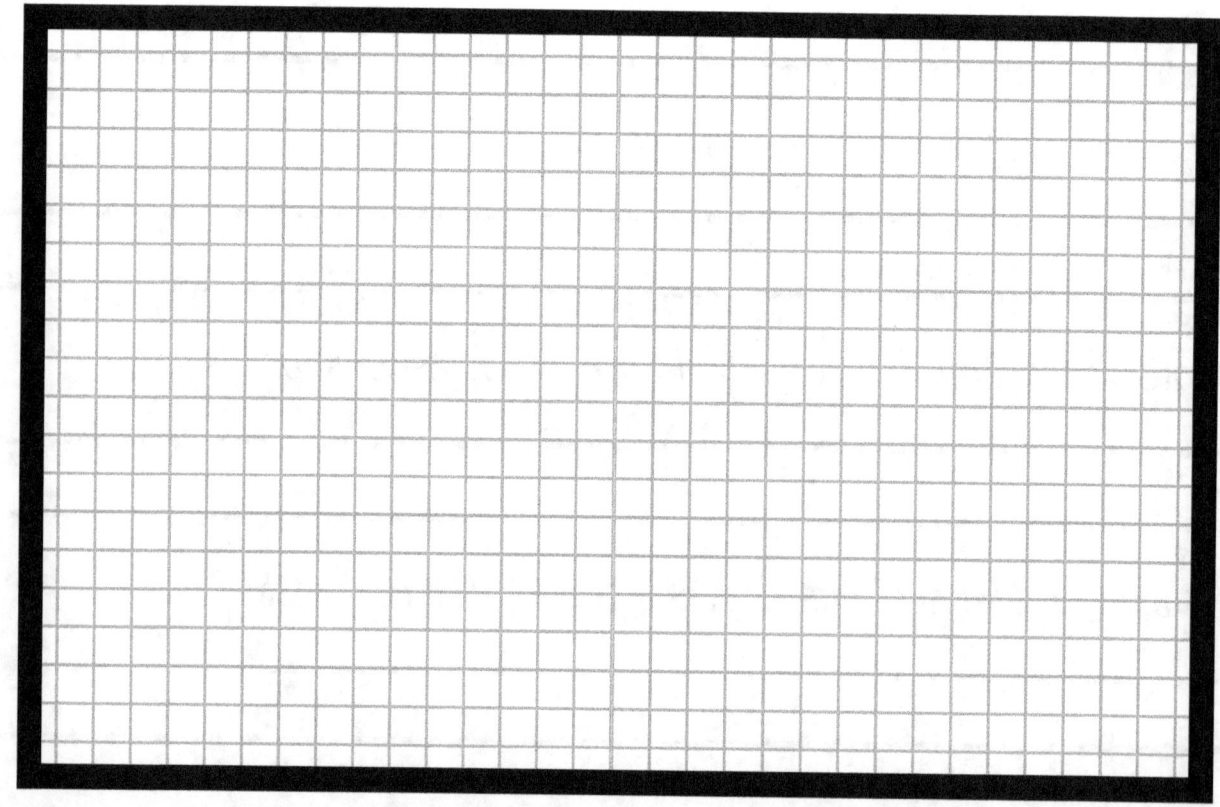

Watering Schedule   S   M   T   W   TH   F   S

Dates

Fertilize:

Mulch:

Prune:

Date of 1st Harvest   __ / __ / __

Type of Fertilizer/Compost   _____

Pest Control   _____

Pruning Notes   _____

_____

Success of Crop/Quantity Harvested

_____

_____

Notes Regarding Success of Planting/Suggestions for Next Year

_____

_____

Unique Challenges This Growing Season (Heat/Frost/Pests)

_____

_____

Seed/Plant Variety _____

Seeds ☐   OR   Starts ☐

Seed Supplier/
Place of Purchase _____

Date Seeds Started ___ / ___ / ___

Quantity Planted _____

Date Starts Planted in Garden ___ / ___ / ___

Intercropping With _____

Garden Bed Layout/Sketch of Planting & Intercropping

Bed # _____

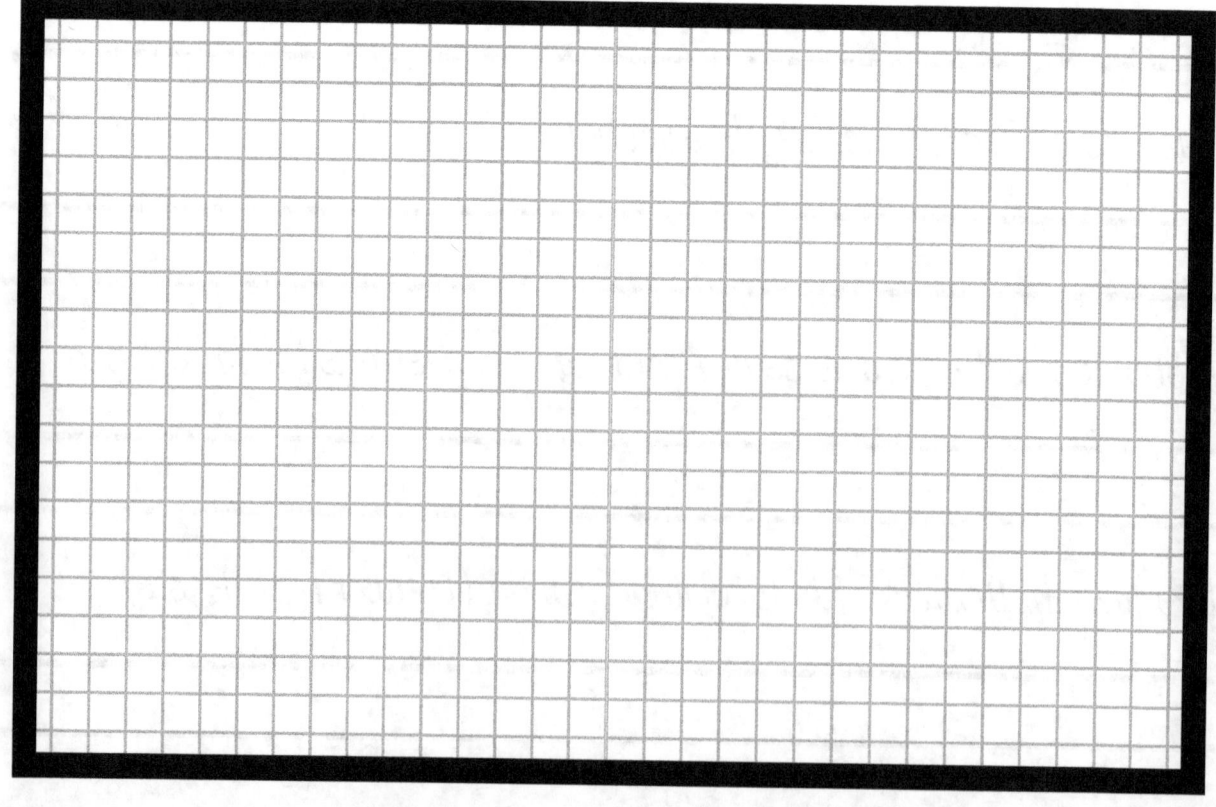

Watering Schedule | S | M | T | W | TH | F | S |

Dates

Fertilize: | | | | | | | | |

Mulch: | | | | | | | | |

Prune: | | | | | | | | |

Date of 1st Harvest   __ / __ / __

Type of Fertilizer/Compost _____

Pest Control _____

Pruning Notes _____

_____

Success of Crop/Quantity Harvested

_____

_____

Notes Regarding Success of Planting/Suggestions for Next Year

_____

_____

Unique Challenges This Growing Season (Heat/Frost/Pests)

_____

_____

Seed/Plant Variety _____

Seeds ☐　OR　Starts ☐

Seed Supplier/
　Place of Purchase　_____

Date Seeds Started　__ / __ / __

Quantity Planted　_____

Date Starts Planted in Garden　__ / __ / __

Intercropping With　_____

Garden Bed Layout/Sketch of Planting & Intercropping

Bed # _____

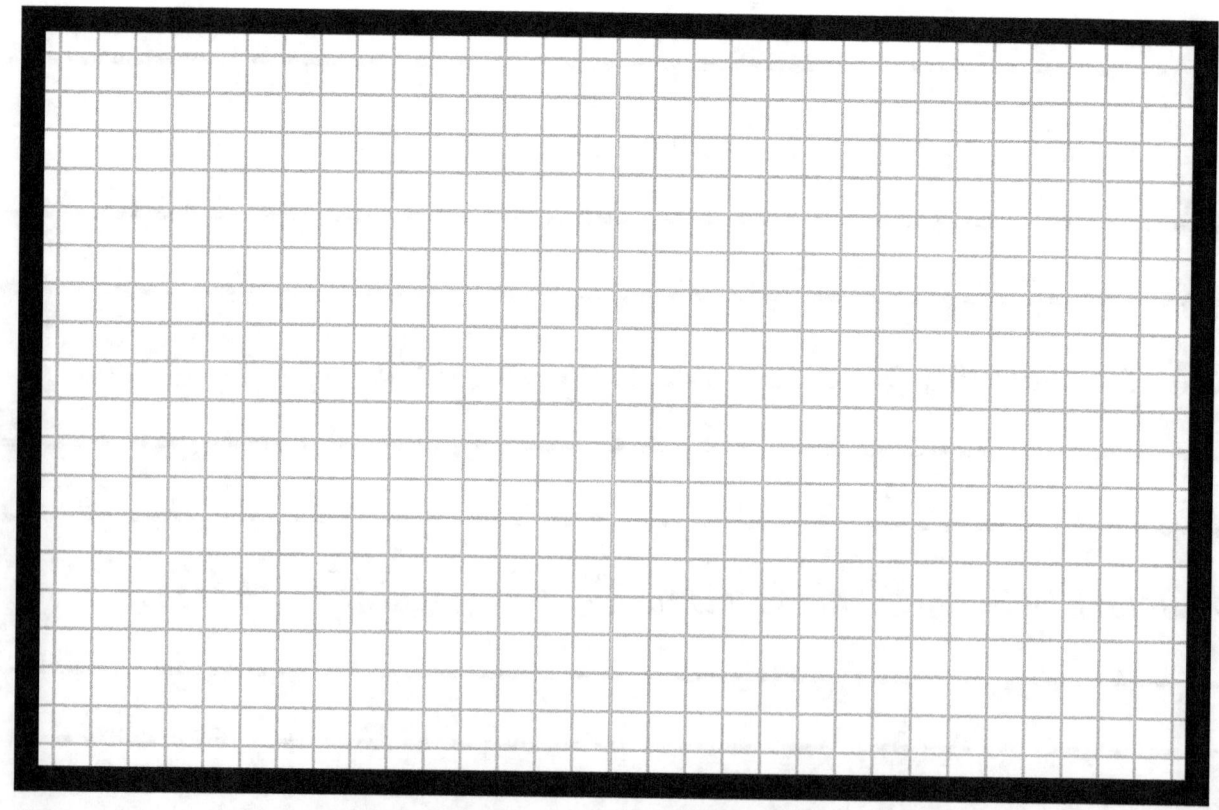

Watering Schedule   S   M   T   W   TH   F   S

Dates

Fertilize:

Mulch:

Prune:

Date of 1st Harvest   __ / __ / __

Type of Fertilizer/Compost _____

Pest Control _____

Pruning Notes _____

_____

Success of Crop/Quantity Harvested

_____

_____

Notes Regarding Success of Planting/Suggestions for Next Year

_____

_____

Unique Challenges This Growing Season (Heat/Frost/Pests)

_____

_____

Seed/Plant Variety _____

Seeds ☐   OR   Starts ☐

Seed Supplier/

Place of Purchase _____

Date Seeds Started __ / __ / __

Quantity Planted _____

Date Starts Planted in Garden __ / __ / __

Intercropping With _____

Garden Bed Layout/Sketch of Planting & Intercropping

Bed # _____

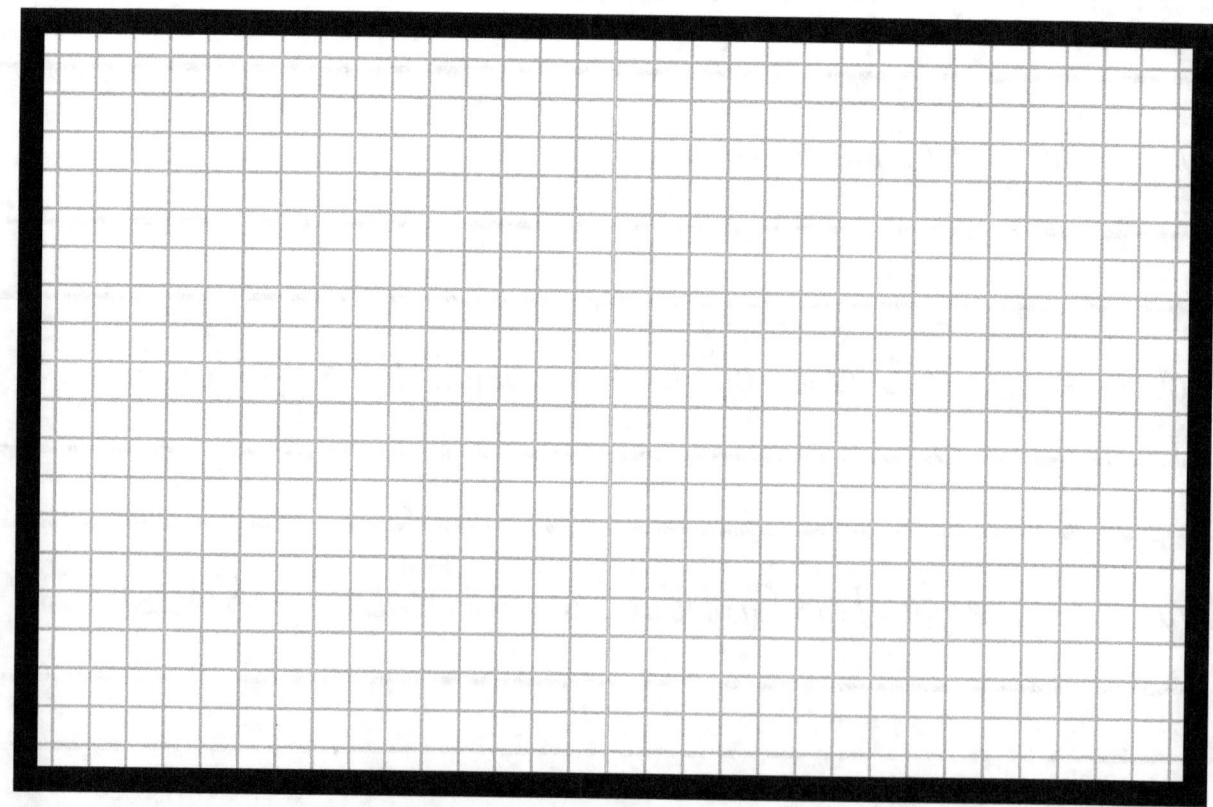

Watering Schedule   [S] [M] [T] [W] [TH] [F] [S]

Dates

Fertilize: | | | | | | | | | | | | | | | |

Mulch: | | | | | | | | | | | | | | | |

Prune: | | | | | | | | | | | | | | | |

Date of 1st Harvest   — / — / —

Type of Fertilizer/Compost _____

Pest Control _____

Pruning Notes _____

_____

Success of Crop/Quantity Harvested

_____

_____

Notes Regarding Success of Planting/Suggestions for Next Year

_____

_____

Unique Challenges This Growing Season (Heat/Frost/Pests)

_____

_____

Seed/Plant Variety _____

Seeds ☐   OR   Starts ☐

Seed Supplier/
   Place of Purchase _____

Date Seeds Started ___ / ___ / ___

Quantity Planted _____

Date Starts Planted in Garden ___ / ___ / ___

Intercropping With _____

Garden Bed Layout/Sketch of Planting & Intercropping
Bed # _____

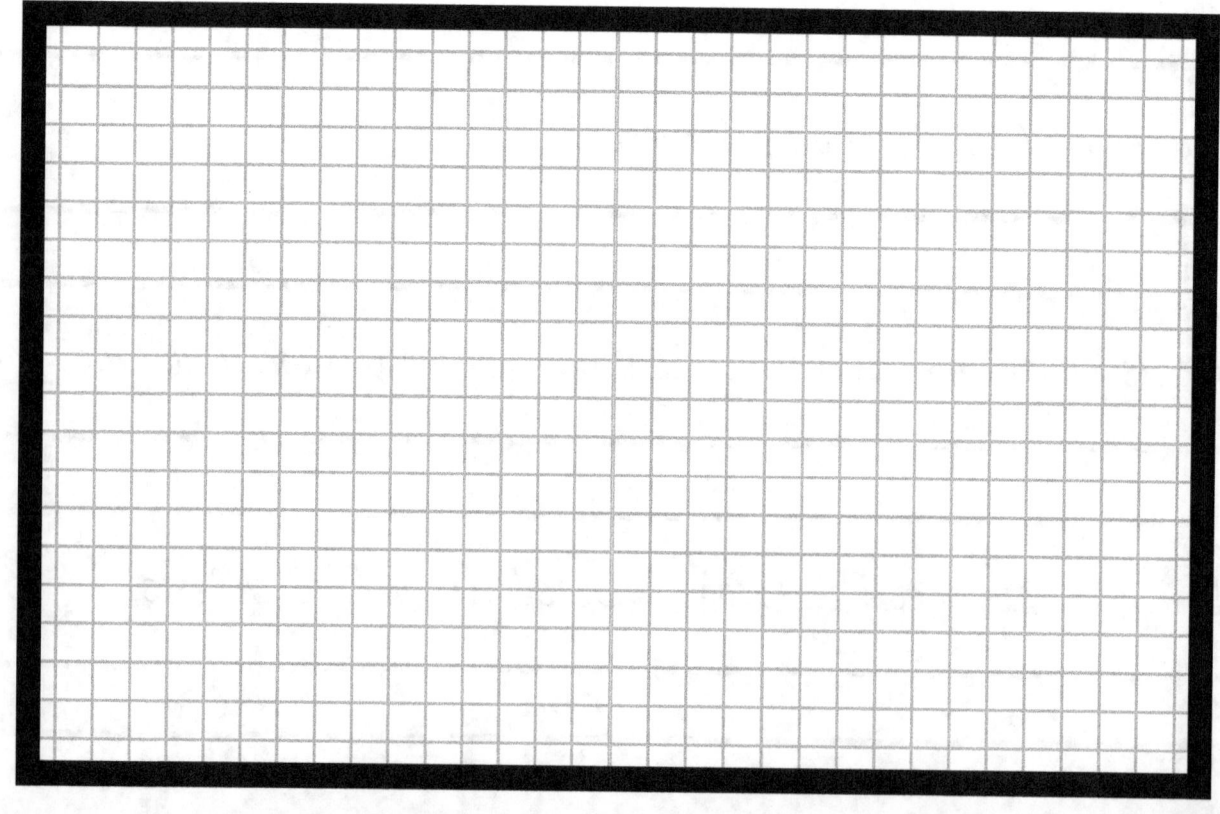

Watering Schedule   ☐S ☐M ☐T ☐W ☐TH ☐F ☐S

Dates

Fertilize:

Mulch:

Prune:

Date of 1st Harvest   —— / —— / ——

Type of Fertilizer/Compost   _____

Pest Control   _____

Pruning Notes   _____

_____

Success of Crop/Quantity Harvested

_____

_____

Notes Regarding Success of Planting/Suggestions for Next Year

_____

_____

Unique Challenges This Growing Season (Heat/Frost/Pests)

_____

_____

Seed/Plant Variety _____

Seeds ☐ OR Starts ☐

Seed Supplier/
  Place of Purchase _____

Date Seeds Started __ / __ / __

Quantity Planted _____

Date Starts Planted in Garden __ / __ / __

Intercropping With _____

Garden Bed Layout/Sketch of Planting & Intercropping

Bed # _____

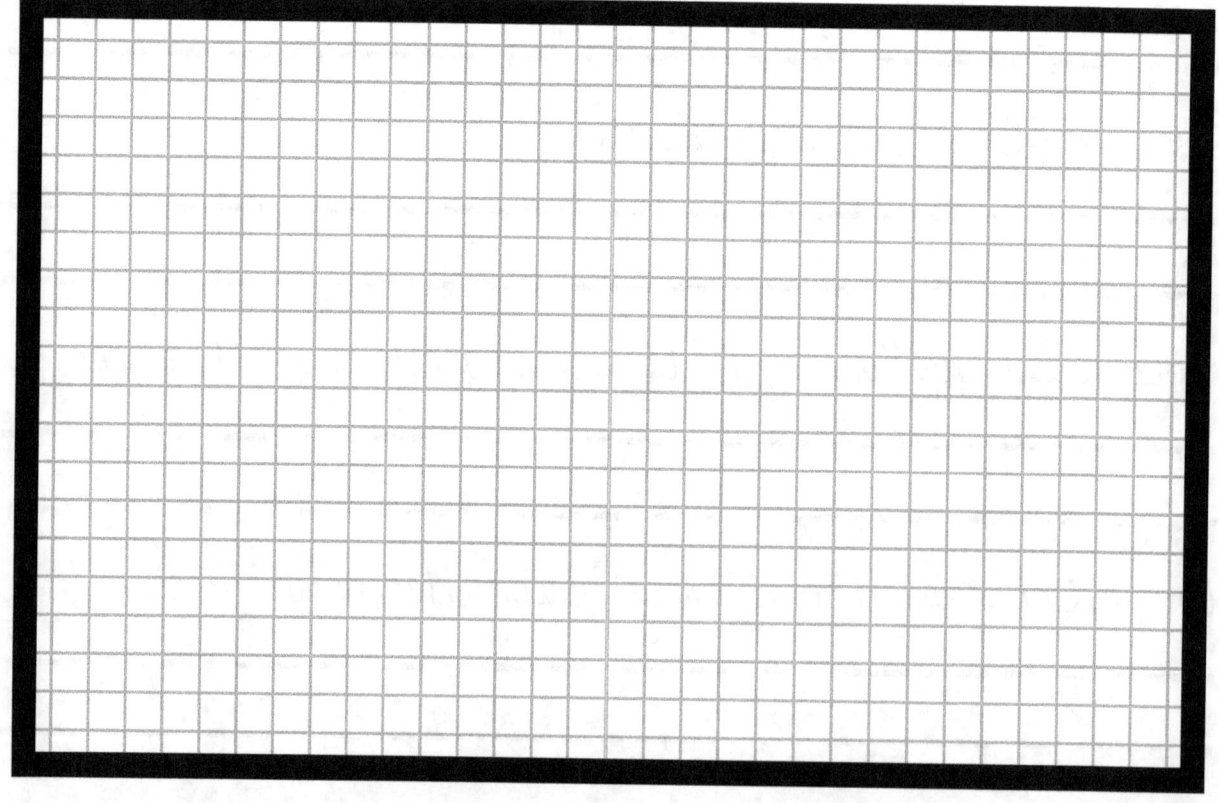

Watering Schedule | S | M | T | W | TH | F | S |

Dates

Fertilize:

Mulch:

Prune:

Date of 1st Harvest   —— / —— / ——

Type of Fertilizer/Compost _____

Pest Control _____

Pruning Notes _____

_____

Success of Crop/Quantity Harvested

_____

_____

Notes Regarding Success of Planting/Suggestions for Next Year

_____

_____

Unique Challenges This Growing Season (Heat/Frost/Pests)

_____

_____

Seed/Plant Variety _____

Seeds ☐   OR   Starts ☐

Seed Supplier/

Place of Purchase _____

Date Seeds Started ___ / ___ / ___

Quantity Planted _____

Date Starts Planted in Garden ___ / ___ / ___

Intercropping With _____

Garden Bed Layout/Sketch of Planting & Intercropping

Bed # _____

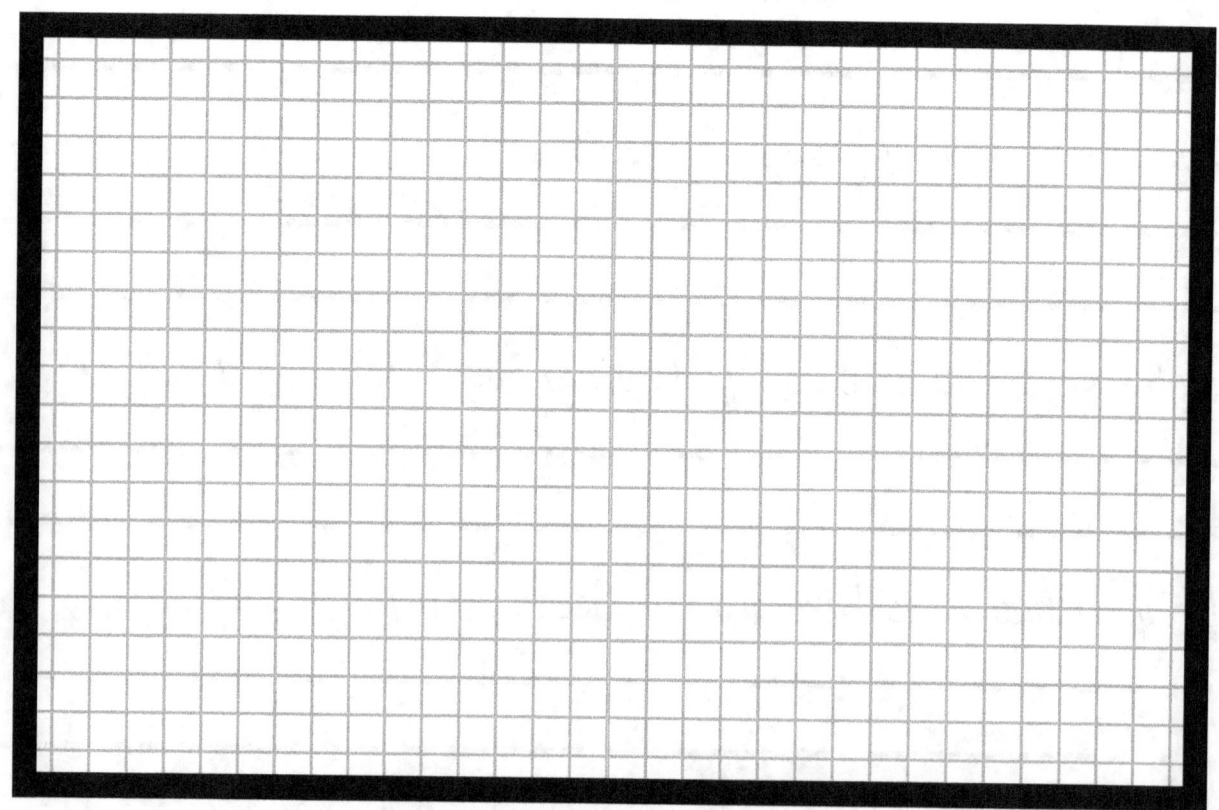

Watering Schedule   S   M   T   W   TH   F   S

Dates

Fertilize:

Mulch:

Prune:

Date of 1st Harvest   —— / —— / ——

Type of Fertilizer/Compost _____

Pest Control _____

Pruning Notes _____

_____

Success of Crop/Quantity Harvested

_____

_____

Notes Regarding Success of Planting/Suggestions for Next Year

_____

_____

Unique Challenges This Growing Season (Heat/Frost/Pests)

_____

_____

Seed/Plant Variety _____

Seeds ☐ OR Starts ☐

Seed Supplier/
Place of Purchase _____

Date Seeds Started __ / __ / __

Quantity Planted _____

Date Starts Planted in Garden __ / __ / __

Intercropping With _____

Garden Bed Layout/Sketch of Planting & Intercropping
Bed # _____

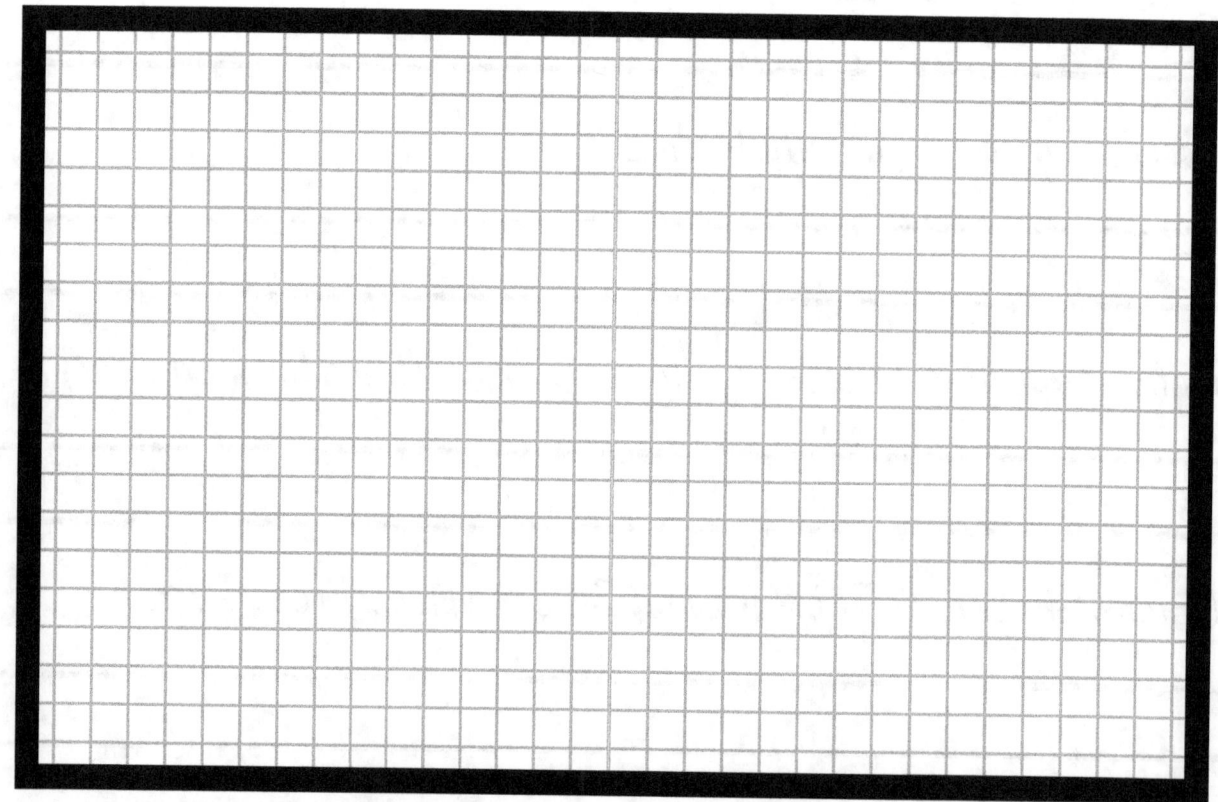

Watering Schedule S M T W TH F S

Dates

Fertilize: | | | | | | | |

Mulch: | | | | | | | |

Prune: | | | | | | | |

Date of 1st Harvest —— / —— / ——

Type of Fertilizer/Compost _____

Pest Control _____

Pruning Notes _____

_____

Success of Crop/Quantity Harvested

_____

_____

Notes Regarding Success of Planting/Suggestions for Next Year

_____

_____

Unique Challenges This Growing Season (Heat/Frost/Pests)

_____

_____

Seed/Plant Variety _____

Seeds ☐ OR Starts ☐

Seed Supplier/
Place of Purchase _____

Date Seeds Started __ / __ / __

Quantity Planted _____

Date Starts Planted in Garden __ / __ / __

Intercropping With _____

Garden Bed Layout/Sketch of Planting & Intercropping
Bed # _____

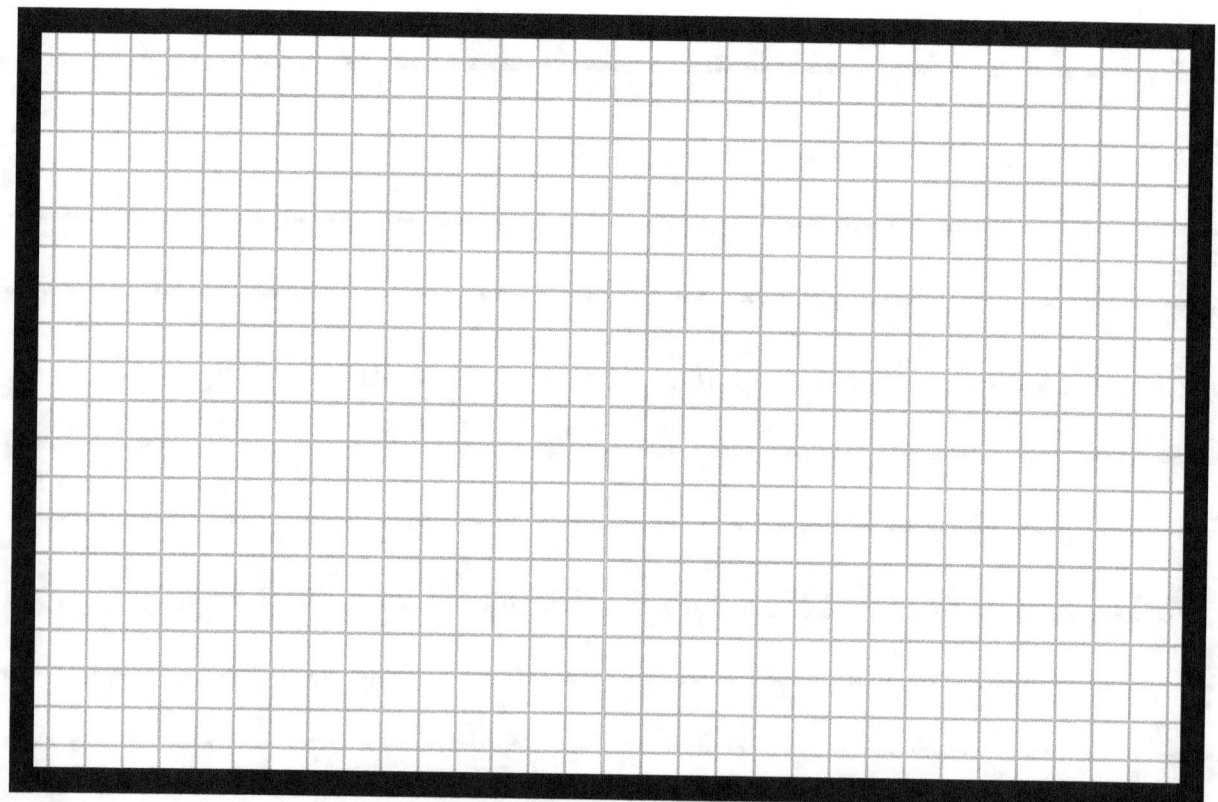

Watering Schedule | S | M | T | W | TH | F | S |

Dates

Fertilize: | | | | | | | | |

Mulch: | | | | | | | | |

Prune: | | | | | | | | |

Date of 1st Harvest ___ / ___ / ___

Type of Fertilizer/Compost _____

Pest Control _____

Pruning Notes _____

_____

Success of Crop/Quantity Harvested

_____

_____

Notes Regarding Success of Planting/Suggestions for Next Year

_____

_____

Unique Challenges This Growing Season (Heat/Frost/Pests)

_____

_____

Seed/Plant Variety _____

Seeds ☐   OR   Starts ☐

Seed Supplier/
  Place of Purchase _____

Date Seeds Started __ / __ / __

Quantity Planted _____

Date Starts Planted in Garden __ / __ / __

Intercropping With _____

Garden Bed Layout/Sketch of Planting & Intercropping

Bed # _____

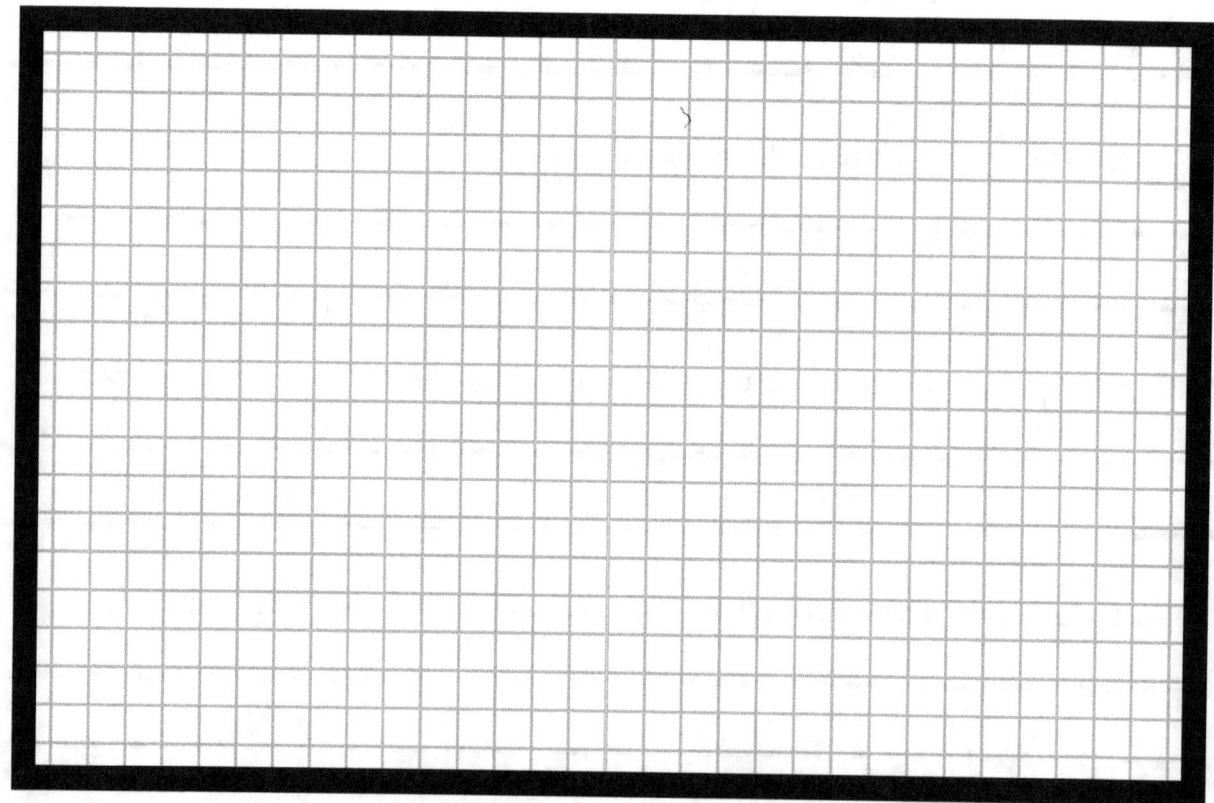

Watering Schedule   S   M   T   W   TH   F   S

Dates

Fertilize: | | | | | | | | |
|---|---|---|---|---|---|---|---|

Mulch: | | | | | | | | |
|---|---|---|---|---|---|---|---|

Prune: | | | | | | | | |
|---|---|---|---|---|---|---|---|

Date of 1st Harvest   — / — / —

Type of Fertilizer/Compost _____

Pest Control _____

Pruning Notes _____

_____

Success of Crop/Quantity Harvested

_____

_____

Notes Regarding Success of Planting/Suggestions for Next Year

_____

_____

Unique Challenges This Growing Season (Heat/Frost/Pests)

_____

_____

Considerations for Next Growing Season

Plans to Rotate Crops

_____

_____

_____

_____

_____

_____

_____

Intercropping Pairings

_____

_____

_____

_____

_____

_____

_____

Considerations for Next Growing Season

New Seed Varieties to Try

_____

_____

_____

_____

_____

_____

Seed & Plant Swap Opportunities

_____

_____

_____

_____

_____

_____

Taking Inventory of Seeds

Leftover Seed Inventory

_____   _____

_____   _____

_____   _____

_____   _____

_____   _____

_____   _____

_____   _____

Seeds to Save From This Year's Garden

_____   _____

_____   _____

_____   _____

_____   _____

_____   _____

_____   _____

Ideas to Explore to Help Extend
My Growing Season

_____

_____

_____

_____

_____

_____

List of Informational Resources i.e. Websites, YouTube Videos, Books, Master Gardeners, Etc.

_____

_____

_____

_____

_____

_____

_____

List of People to Crop Share With

_____
_____
_____
_____

Places to Donate Excess Crops

_____
_____
_____
_____
_____

Garden Volunteer Opportunities & Community Gardens

_____
_____
_____

Notes

Notes